Ecosystems

 HOUGHTON MIFFLIN

BOSTON

Printed in the U.S.A.   ISBN-13: 978-0-547-06224-2   ISBN-10: 0-547-06224-9   2 3 4 5 6 7 8 9-VH-16 15 14 13 12 11 10 09 08

You Can...

Do What Scientists Do

Meet Dr. Kenneth Sulak. He works for the United States Geological Survey. He studies fish and other animals that live deep in the ocean. Dr. Sulak wants to find out what kinds of animals live far below the surface. He wants to know how many of them there are and how they live. He also wants to know how deep-sea animals interact with animals in the shallower water above them.

Dr. Sulak's research depends on submersibles. A ship with a crane lowers a sub into the Gulf of Mexico. In it, Dr. Sulak can travel far below the surface to observe and collect deep-sea life.

Ocean fishing, exploring for oil, and other human activities are moving into deeper and deeper water. Dr. Sulak helps keep track of how these activities affect deep-sea life. He shares what he learns by speaking to and answering the questions of other scientists. He also writes about it in science magazines.

Scientists investigate in different ways.

The ways scientists investigate depend on the questions they ask. Dr. Sulak observes animals in their natural habitats. He also classifies animals. Often, he measures water temperatures. Other scientists ask questions that can be answered by doing a fair test called an experiment.

Dr. Kenneth Sulak uses a microscope to learn more about deep-sea life. He has been surprised to discover how many animals live very deep in the ocean and that many deep-sea animals are bright red.

Think Like a Scientist

The ways scientists ask and answer questions about the world around them is called **scientific inquiry.** Scientific inquiry requires certain attitudes, or ways of thinking. To think like a scientist you have to be:

- curious and ask a lot of questions.

- creative and think up new ways to do things.

- able to keep an open mind. That means you listen to the ideas of others.

- open to changing what you think when your investigation results surprise you.

- willing to question what other people tell you.

Tides are changes in the level of the ocean that occur each day. What causes tides?

Use Critical Thinking

When you think critically you make decisions about what others tell you or what you read. Is what you heard or read fact or opinion? A *fact* can be checked to make sure it is true. An *opinion* is what you think about the facts.

Did anyone ever tell you how something works that you found hard to believe? When you ask, "What facts back up your idea?" you are thinking critically. Critical thinkers question scientific statements.

Tides seem to rise and fall at about the same time each day. I wonder what causes tides to keep changing that way?

I read that tides are caused by the pull of the Moon's gravity on Earth's oceans. The level of the oceans keeps rising and falling as the Moon and Earth move into different positions.

Science Inquiry

Using scientific inquiry helps you understand the world around you. For example, suppose you collect a sample of water from the ocean and put it in the freezer over night.

Observe The next day, you notice that the ocean water is not completely frozen. You also notice that ice cubes in the freezer are frozen solid.

Ask a Question When you think about what you saw, heard, or read, you may have questions.

Hypothesis Think about facts you already know. Do you have an idea about the answer? Write it down. That is your hypothesis.

Experiment Plan a test that will tell if the hypothesis is true or not. List the materials and tools you will need. Write the steps you will follow. Make sure that you keep all conditions the same except the one you are testing. That condition is called the *variable.*

Conclusion What do your results tell you? Do they support your hypothesis or show it to be false?

Describe your experiment with enough detail that others can repeat it. Communicate your results and conclusion.

My Salt Water Experiment

Observe It seems that ocean water does not freeze at the same temperature as plain water. Ocean water is salty.

Ask a question How does salt affect the freezing point of water?

Hypothesis Plain water will freeze before salt water because it has a higher freezing point than salt water.

Experiment I will put labeled containers of the same amount of salt water and plain water in a freezer. I will check on the containers every 3 minutes. I will record in which container the water freezes first.

Conclusion Plain water turns to ice before salt water. The results support my hypothesis. Plain water has a higher freezing point than salt water.

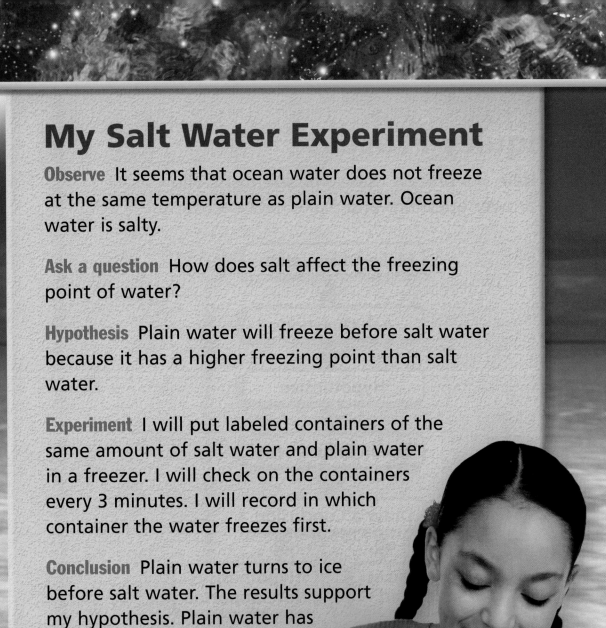

Inquiry Process

Here is a process that some scientists follow to answer questions and make new discoveries.

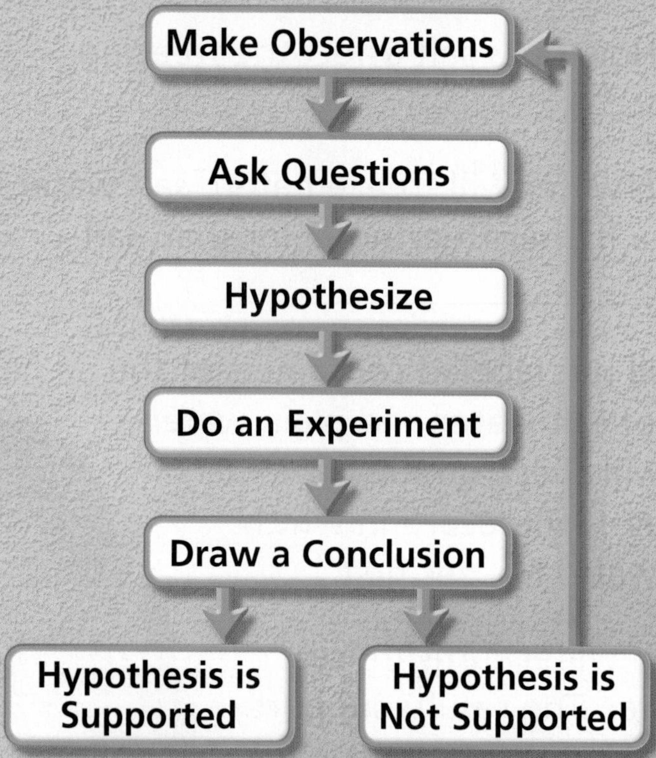

Make Observations

↓

Ask Questions

↓

Hypothesize

↓

Do an Experiment

↓

Draw a Conclusion

↓

Hypothesis is Supported   **Hypothesis is Not Supported**

Science Inquiry Skills

You'll use many of these inquiry skills when you investigate and experiment.

- Ask Questions
- Observe
- Compare
- Classify
- Predict
- Measure

- Hypothesize
- Use Variables
- Experiment
- Use Models
- Communicate
- Use Numbers

- Record Data
- Analyze Data
- Infer
- Collaborate
- Research

Try It Yourself!

Experiment With an Energy Sphere

When you touch both metal strips of the Energy Sphere, the sphere lights. This works with two people—as long as they are in contact with one another.

1 What questions do you have about the Energy Sphere?

2 How would you find out the answers?

3 Write your experiment plan and predict what will happen.

You Can...

Be an Inventor

Alberto Behar's interest in space led him to a career in space engineering. Dr. Behar helped to invent a new kind of Martian rover. Called the tumbleweed, it looks more like a giant beach ball than a vehicle. It moves when the wind blows it.

The idea for the tumbleweed came about by accident. During a test of a rover with large inflatable wheels, one of the wheels fell off. The wind blew the wheel several kilometers before someone caught it. The idea of a wind-blown rover was born.

The tumbleweed has performed very well in tests on Earth. Dr. Behar thinks it may soon be used to explore the surface of Mars.

"When I was about seven or eight, I wanted to be an astronaut. I checked out all of the books on space I could at the library..."

What Is Technology?

The tools people make and the things they build with tools are all **technology.** A toy car is technology. So is a race car.

Scientists use technology, too. For example, a laser beam can be used to make very precise measurements. Scientists also use microscopes to see things they cannot see with just their eyes.

Many technologies make the world a better place to live. But sometimes a technology that solves one problem can cause other problems. For example, farmers use fertilizer to increase the yields of their crops. But fertilizer can be carried by rain water into lakes and streams where it can harm fish and other living things.

A Better Idea

"I wish I had a better way to _____." How would you fill in the blank? Everyone wishes they could find a way to do their jobs more easily or have more fun. Inventors try to make those wishes come true. Inventing or improving an invention requires time and patience.

George Hansburg patented the pogo stick in 1919. It was a Y-shaped metal stick with two foot rests and a spring. Today's pogo sticks are not much different.

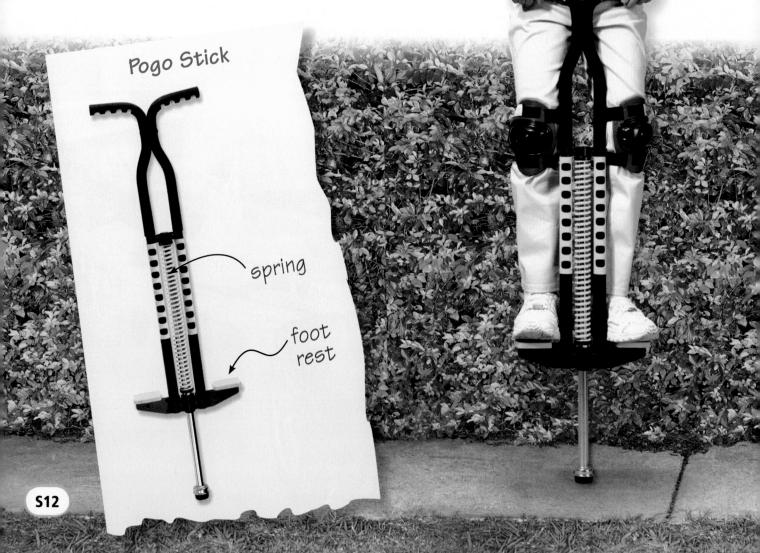

Pogo Stick

spring

foot rest

How to Be an Inventor

1. **Identify a problem.** It may be a problem at school, at home, or in your community.

2. **List ways to solve the problem.** Sometimes the solution is a new tool. Other times it may be a new way of doing an old job or activity.

3. **Choose the best solution.** Decide which idea you predict will work best. Think about which one you can carry out.

4. **Make a sample.** A sample, called a *prototype*, is the first try. Your idea may need many materials or none at all. Choose measuring tools that will help your design work better.

5. **Try out your invention.** Use your prototype, or ask someone else to try it. Keep a record of how it works and what problems you find. The more times you try it, the more information you will have.

6. **Improve your invention.** Use what you learned to make your design work better. Draw or write about the changes you make and why you made them.

7. **Share your invention.** Show your invention to others. Explain how it works. Tell how it makes an activity easier or more fun. If it did not work as well as you wanted, tell why.

Make Decisions

Trouble for the Everglades

For many years, the water of the Florida Everglades has had too much phosphorus. The phosphorus comes from nearby farms and cities. Phosphorus in fertilizers washes into streams and rivers. Phosphorus in laundry detergents washes down drains. Much of the phosphorus ends up in the water of the Everglades.

Some types of plants and animals have not been able to stand the high phosphorus levels. They have decreased in numbers or even gone extinct. Scientists are trying to reduce the amount of phosphorus entering the Everglades. They are also looking for ways to remove the phosphorus that is already there.

Deciding What to Do

What methods are best to help lower phosphorus levels in the water of the Everglades?

Here's how to make your decision about the phosphorus problem. You can use the same steps to help solve problems in your home, in your school, and in your community.

Learn → Learn about the problem. Take the time needed to get the facts. You could talk to an expert, read a science book, or explore a web site.

List → Make a list of actions you could take. Add actions other people could take.

Decide → Think about each action on your list. Decide which choice is the best one for you or your community.

Share → Communicate your decision to others.

Phosphorus In The Everglades

Sources of Phosphorus
- Fertilizers
- Detergents
- Other Sources

Phosphorus Level

Year

Solutions

fertilizer

Science Safety

☑ Know the safety rules of your school and classroom and follow them.

☑ Read and follow the safety tips in each Investigation activity.

☑ When you plan your own investigations, write down how to keep safe.

☑ Know how to clean up and put away science materials. Keep your work area clean and tell your teacher about spills right away.

☑ Know how to safely plug in electrical devices.

☑ Wear safety goggles when your teacher tells you.

☑ Unless your teacher tells you to, never put any science materials in or near your ears, eyes, or mouth.

☑ Wear gloves when handling live animals.

☑ Wash your hands when your investigation is done.

Caring for Living Things

☑ Learn how to care for the plants and animals in your classroom so that they stay healthy and safe. Learn how to hold animals carefully.

LIFE  SCIENCE

UNIT B

Ecosystems

Ecosystems

Independent Reading

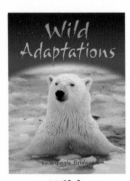

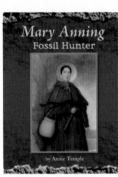

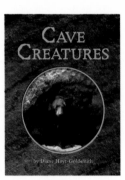

Wild Adaptations

Mary Anning Fossil Hunter

Cave Creatures

Discover!

Corals look like colorful plants but they are tiny ocean animals. Over time, some kinds of coral build huge coral reefs. How old can coral reefs be? You will have the answer to this question by the end of the unit.

Chapter 5

Parts of Ecosystems

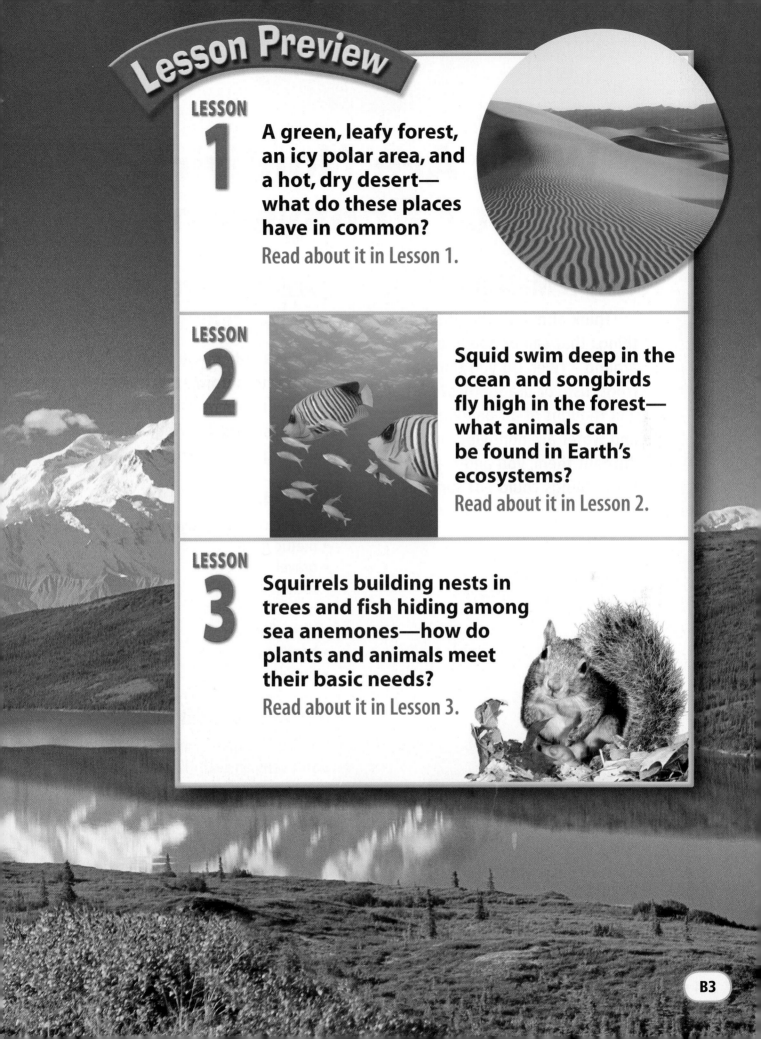

Lesson Preview

LESSON 1

A green, leafy forest, an icy polar area, and a hot, dry desert— what do these places have in common?

Read about it in Lesson 1.

LESSON 2

Squid swim deep in the ocean and songbirds fly high in the forest— what animals can be found in Earth's ecosystems?

Read about it in Lesson 2.

LESSON 3

Squirrels building nests in trees and fish hiding among sea anemones—how do plants and animals meet their basic needs?

Read about it in Lesson 3.

What Are Nonliving Parts of Ecosystems?

Why It Matters...

Think about all the different things that can be found in and around a river. Do you think of frogs, fish, or dragonflies? Perhaps you thought of air and water. Air and water are nonliving things. Without them, you and many other living things could not survive.

PREPARE TO INVESTIGATE

Inquiry Skill

Observe When you observe, you gather information about the environment using your five senses: seeing, hearing, smelling, touching, and tasting.

Materials

- plastic container (terrarium) with lid
- metric ruler
- gravel
- rocks
- potting soil
- dish of water
- hand lens
- goggles

Science and Math Toolbox

For step 1, review **Using a Hand Lens** on page H2.

Life Support

Procedure

1. **Observe** Use a hand lens to examine the nonliving gravel, soil, rocks, and water.

2. **Measure** Fill a plastic container with a layer of gravel about 2 centimeters deep. Then add a layer of soil about 5 centimeters deep on top of the gravel. Use a ruler to measure.
Safety: Wear goggles when adding gravel and soil to the container.

3. Place rocks and a shallow dish of water in the container. Put the lid on.

4. **Record Data** In your *Science Notebook*, list all the nonliving things in the container. Include those you can see and any that you know are there but cannot see. Make a drawing of each thing you see. Label your drawings.

Conclusion

1. **Compare** Compare your list with another student's list. How are they similar? How are they different?

2. **Infer** What types of plants and animals do you think could live in your container? Give reasons for your choices.

3. **Predict** How would these living things interact with the nonliving things in the container?

STEP 2

STEP 3

STEP 4

Nonliving Things

rock

Investigate More!

Research Do research to find out what nonliving things can be found in Antarctica. What kinds of living things are found in this environment?

VOCABULARY

ecosystem	p. B6
organic matter	p. B6
soil	p. B6

READING SKILL

Classify Use a chart to show the nonliving parts of a desert ecosystem and a polar ecosystem.

Nonliving Things in Ecosystems

MAIN IDEA Nonliving parts of an ecosystem, such as water, air, and sunlight, help living things meet their basic needs.

Ecosystems and Nonliving Things

Look out the window and you'll see an ecosystem (EE koh sihs tuhm). An **ecosystem** is made up of all the living and nonliving things that interact in an area. Nonliving things in ecosystems can include water, air, soil, and light. Nonliving things help living things meet their needs.

Soil is the loose material that covers much of Earth's surface. It is made up of tiny pieces of rocks, minerals, and organic (awr GAN ihk) matter. Most plants grow best in soil that contains a lot of organic matter. **Organic matter**, the remains of plants and animals, is rich in nutrients, or materials that help living things grow.

Both plants and animals depend on sunlight. Plants need sunlight to make food. Some plants and animals can only survive in warm temperatures. Others grow better in the shade provided by trees, such as those found in a forest. Shade protects a living thing from direct sunlight and high temperatures.

CLASSIFY What are some nonliving parts of an ecosystem?

A Forest Ecosystem

Light Plants need light to make food.

Air Both plants and animals need air to carry out their life processes.

Water A stream provides needed water for some of the animals and plants in the forest.

Shade Some organisms thrive in the shade offered by trees.

Soil Soil on the forest floor provides plants with the support and nutrients they need to grow.

Different Ecosystems

Each ecosystem has its own set of nonliving parts which includes light, water, temperature, and soil. These conditions determine the kinds of living things that are able to survive in that ecosystem. A living thing can survive only where its needs are met.

A Polar Ecosystem

Ice covers the land surface in a polar ecosystem. Temperatures are very low. During half the year, there is little or no sunlight. Even in this harsh place, there are animals that live and meet their needs. Polar bears are among them. With layers of fat and thick fur, these animals are able to keep warm. For food the bears hunt animals that live in ocean water under and around the ice.

A Desert Ecosystem

In a desert ecosystem, daytime temperatures are very high. There is very little rainfall. The soil is sandy and has few nutrients. Desert plants and animals must be able to adapt to these conditions. For example, the saltbush plant sends its roots deep into the ground to collect water. Many desert animals are active only at night when temperatures are lower.

▶ **CLASSIFY** What conditions would you find in a polar ecosystem?

Visual Summary

Ecosystems are made up of living and nonliving things.

Different ecosystems have different light, soil, water, and temperature conditions.

The light, soil, water, and temperature conditions in an ecosystem determine which plants and animals can live there.

LINKS for Home and School

MATH Measuring Air Each 100 liters of air you breathe is made up of 79 liters of nitrogen and other gases. The rest is oxygen. Your lungs only use oxygen. How much oxygen will your lungs get from 100 liters of air?

TECHNOLOGY Name Nonliving Parts Choose an invention, such as an automobile. Name all of the nonliving things you can think of that the invention uses. Where in the environment did those things come from?

Review

B9

1 MAIN IDEA How do some of the nonliving parts of an ecosystem help a plant or animal meet its needs?

2 VOCABULARY Use the term *organic matter* in a sentence about soil.

3 READING SKILL: Classify Use a chart to show living and nonliving parts of a desert ecosystem.

4 CRITICAL THINKING: Analyze What is the relationship between living and nonliving parts of an ecosystem?

5 INQUIRY SKILL: Observe Look at the forest ecosystem on page B7. Identify all the nonliving parts.

 TEST PREP

The nonliving parts of an ecosystem ___.

A. are the same in every ecosystem

B. determine which plants and animals can live in the ecosystem

C. include animals and plants

D. do not interact with the living parts of an ecosystem

 Technology
Visit **www.eduplace.com/scp/** to find more about the nonliving parts of ecosystems.

What Are Living Parts of Ecosystems?

Why It Matters...

Every ecosystem is home to its own set of plants and animals. The environment provides the organisms with the things they need to survive. This colorful bird, for example, lives in the trees of the Amazon rainforest. The rainforest provides all the food, water, and shelter the bird needs.

PREPARE TO INVESTIGATE

Inquiry Skill

Research When you do research, you learn more about a subject by looking in books, searching the Internet, or asking science experts.

Materials

- resource materials
- plastic container (terrarium) from Lesson 1
- grass and moss plants
- earthworms
- crickets
- apple slices
- cotton balls

Science and Math Toolbox

For step 1, review **Making a Chart to Organize Data** on page H10.

Right at Home
Procedure

1. **Research** In your *Science Notebook*, make a chart like the one shown. Use resource materials provided by your teacher to help you complete the *Basic Needs* column.

2. **Experiment** Use the container from the Lesson 1 Investigate. Plant grass and moss plants firmly in the soil. Place a few earthworms and crickets in the container along with an apple slice. Refresh the water in the dish and add cotton balls to it. Then replace the lid. You have made a terrarium (tuh RAIR ee uhm), or a model of an ecosystem. Put it in sunlight.

3. **Observe** Several times a day observe the living things to see how they meet their needs. Record your observations. Change the water and cotton balls and add apple slices when necessary.

Conclusion

1. **Compare** Exchange charts with another student. How are your charts similar? How are they different?

2. **Predict** Choose one of the nonliving things in your terrarium. If this nonliving thing were removed, what effect would this have on the living things? Would each living thing still be able to meet its needs? Explain your answer.

STEP 1

Living Thing	Basic Needs	How It Meets Needs
grass		
moss		
worm		
cricket		

STEP 2

STEP 3

Investigate More!
Design an Experiment
Plan an experiment to find out how an animal in a nearby ecosystem meets its needs. With your teacher's permission, observe the animal outside.

VOCABULARY

community	p. B12
environment	p. B12
population	p. B12
prairie	p. B14
rainforest	p. B14
temperate zone	p. B15

READING SKILL

Cause and Effect Use a chart to show the effect that nonliving parts of an ecosystem have on the living things in that ecosystem.

Living Things in Ecosystems

MAIN IDEA Different ecosystems are home to different kinds of living things.

Communities and Populations

Recall that ecosystems are made up of all the living and nonliving things in an area. A forest ecosystem contains many kinds of living things. That's because many kinds of plants and animals can find the things they need to survive there.

A living thing will survive only in an environment (ehn VY ruhn muhnt) that meets its needs. An **environment** is everything that surrounds and affects a living thing.

All the living things in an ecosystem make up a **community** (kuh MYOO nih tee). Within a community, there are different populations (pahp-yuh LAY shuhnz) of living things. A **population** is all the members of one kind of plant or animal in a community. So all the white-tailed deer in the forest community are one population. All the trillium in the forest are a plant population.

▶ **CAUSE AND EFFECT** Explain why forest ecosystems support so many kinds of plants and animals.

A Forest Ecosystem

Warblers use forest trees for shelter.

Deer rely on grasses and tree leaves for food.

Beavers use trees to build lodges for shelter.

Trillium plants grow best in shady areas and damp soils.

The Right Ecosystem

A **rainforest** (RAYN fawr ihst) is an area where it rains a lot. In many rainforests it is warm all year and there is a lot of sunlight. In the rainforest of Washington State, temperatures are mild. Trees there tend to grow close together. This dense forest provides shelter and water for many kinds of animals.

A **prairie** (PRAIR ee) is a grassy land area with few or no trees. Prairies receive more rainfall than deserts, but less than forests. Winters are cold, and summers are hot. Grasses grow well here.

The prairie ecosystem is home to animals that feed on grasses and their seeds. There are few trees in a prairie. Many prairie animals make their homes underground.

rainforest ecosystem

prairie ecosystem

Some Ecosystems in the United States

WASHINGTON

SOUTH DAKOTA

There are ecosystems in cities. New York City's Central Park is home for many plants and animals. New York City is located in a temperate (TEHM pur iht) zone. A **temperate zone** is an area of the Earth where the temperature rarely gets very hot or very cold. Many kinds of plants and animals can meet their needs in such a place.

In the Florida Everglades, most of the land is covered by water. The trees and tall grasses grow from the muddy bottom of the shallow water. Water plants and tiny algae live in the water. These organisms are food for animals such as shrimp and fish. Wading birds, such as herons and egrets, eat the animals that live in the water.

▶ **CAUSE AND EFFECT** **Why do many prairie animals make their homes underground?**

ecosystem in a city park

Florida Everglades ecosystem

Conditions in Ecosystems

A terrarium is a model ecosystem. In a terrarium, living parts of an ecosystem interact with each other and with nonliving parts. Different parts of the ecosystem have slightly different conditions. In the terrarium shown, the rock and twigs under the heat lamp are dry and warm. The soil under the ferns is moist and cool. Like the terrarium, large ecosystems have conditions that vary in different areas. Organisms live where the conditions best meet their needs.

In the ocean, conditions vary in a coral reef ecosystem. Some organisms meet their needs at the top of the reef, near the water's surface. Others live in deeper water. The reef is made of living and nonliving parts of tiny coral animals. These animals produce a hard outer casing. When they die, their stony casing remains. Over time new coral grow on the casings, forming the reef.

▶ **CAUSE AND EFFECT** How can conditions within the same terrarium ecosystem be different?

Terrarium Ecosystem

ferns growing in soil

lizards getting heat from lamp

Visual Summary

All the different populations of plants and animals living in one area make up a community.

Every ecosystem has its own set of nonliving conditions. Living things that live there are suited to those conditions.

Different areas of an ecosystem have different conditions. Organisms live in the conditions that best meet their needs.

LINKS for Home and School

WRITING Story In the past, ecosystems affected the kind of transportation used. Camels were used in deserts, dogsleds in arctic areas. People still use some of these methods of transportation. Write a story about an imaginary journey through an ecosystem using an unusual method of transportation.

ART Make a Diorama A diorama can use many materials to create a scene. Create a diorama of an ecosystem. You may use things such as light, water, and music along with typical art materials.

Review

1 MAIN IDEA How do living things in an ecosystem interact?

2 VOCABULARY Define the term *environment*.

3 READING SKILL: Cause and Effect What might happen if all the trees in a forest ecosystem were cut down?

4 CRITICAL THINKING: Apply Describe an ecosystem in which conditions are slightly different in different areas of the ecosystem.

5 INQUIRY SKILL: Research Use resource materials to research a rainforest ecosystem. Why do so few plants grow on the rainforest floor?

 TEST PREP

A community is made up of ___.

A. all the living things in an ecosystem

B. all the nonliving things in an ecosystem

C. all the living and nonliving things in an ecosystem

D. all the members of one kind of plant or animal

 Technology
Visit **www.eduplace.com/scp/** to read more about different kinds of ecosystems.

Read a selection from *Midnight Fox* about a boy searching for the den of a black fox. Then compare it to a table from *Crafty Canines*. The table gives information about five other kinds of fox.

The Midnight Fox
by Betsy Byars

Tom spies a fox in a woody area. Suddenly, he is caught up with tracking this mysterious fox.

For the past two weeks I had been practically tearing the woods apart looking for the den of the black fox. I had poked under rocks and logs and stuck sticks in rotted trees, and it was a wonder that some animal had not come storming out....

After a while I looked across the creek and I saw a hollow where there was a small clearing. There was an outcropping of rocks behind the clearing and an old log slanted against the rocks. Soft grass sloped down to the creek bank.

I don't know how long I sat there—I usually forgot about my watch when I was in the woods—but it was a long time. I was just sitting, not expecting anything or waiting for anything. And the black fox came through the bushes.

She...gave a small yapping bark, and at once, out of a hole beneath rocks came a baby fox.

Crafty Canines: Coyotes, Foxes, and Wolves
by Phyllis J. Perry

There are twenty kinds of foxes. Climate and terrain influence where a fox lives. Most of the time, a fox makes its den in an empty rabbit hole or other burrow. If there are no burrows, a fox might dig one.

Fox	Habitat
Red fox	Open fields and woodlands in Asia, Europe, the Middle East, Canada, and throughout the United States
Kit fox	Deserts of the southwestern United States, northern Mexico, and Baja California
Bat-eared fox	Open grasslands and semideserts of eastern and northern Africa, and from Southern Angola and Zimbabwe to South Africa
Crab-eating fox	Woodlands and savannahs of Colombia, Venezuela, Brazil, Guyana, Suriname, eastern Peru, Bolivia, Paraguay, Argentina, and Uruguay
Arctic fox	Along the coast of Greenland and in the northern sections of Canada, Alaska, Iceland, Scandinavia, and Siberia

Sharing Ideas

1. **READING CHECK** In *The Midnight Fox*, where does Tom discover the baby fox?

2. **WRITE ABOUT IT** Make a chart comparing and contrasting the habitat of the Arctic fox and the habitat described in *The Midnight Fox*.

3. **TALK ABOUT IT** Discuss the living and nonliving parts of the ecosystem described in *The Midnight Fox*.

What Are Some Roles of Living Things?

Why It Matters...

In all ecosystems animals depend on plants for food and shelter. The monarch butterfly lays eggs on the underside of the leaves of the milkweed plant. When the monarch caterpillars hatch, they feed on these leaves.

PREPARE TO INVESTIGATE

Inquiry Skill

Analyze Data You can use the data in charts, graphs, or diagrams to make inferences and predictions.

Materials

- terrarium from Lesson 2
- hand lens

Science and Math Toolbox

For step 2, review **Using a Hand Lens** on page H2.

Organisms Interact
Procedure

1 **Record Data** In your *Science Notebook*, make a chart like the one shown.

2 **Observe** Use a hand lens to look closely at the grass, moss, worms, and crickets in the terrarium. Record your observations in your chart.

3 **Experiment** Place the terrarium in the shade, away from sunlight. Allow it to remain in the shade for 2 or 3 days. Add apple slices and water and change the cotton balls as needed. **Safety:** Handle the terrarium carefully so you do not disturb the plants and animals.

4 **Observe** Look closely again at the living things in the terrarium. Record your observations in your chart.

Conclusion

1. **Analyze Data** Look at your chart. What, if any, changes did you observe in the grass and crickets? What, if any, earthworm activity did you see?

2. **Infer** In what ways do animals depend on plants in their ecosystem?

3. **Hypothesize** In what ways might plants depend on animals in their ecosystem?

STEP 1

	With Sunlight	Without Sunlight
grass		
moss		
worm		
crickets		

STEP 2

STEP 3

Investigate More!
Solve a Problem

Bluebirds no longer nest near your school. They built their nests in holes in trees but those trees have been cut down. What can you or your community do to bring back the bluebirds?

VOCABULARY

consumer	p. B24
pollinator	p. B26
producer	p. B24
reproduction	p. B26
seed dispersal	p. B26

READING SKILL

Main Ideas and Details
Use a chart to show details that support the idea that animals depend on one another.

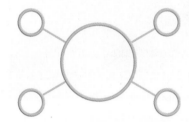

Roles of Living Things

MAIN IDEA Living things in an ecosystem depend on one another for basic needs such as food, shelter, and protection.

Interdependence

The living things found in an ecosystem are interdependent (ihn tur dih PEHN duhnt). This means that living things depend on each other to meet their needs. You know that many animals depend on plants for food. But organisms depend on each other for other things, too.

Plants can be a source of shelter for animals. In turn, animals can provide protection for plants. The swollen thorn acacia tree and a type of stinging ant are interdependent. The ants live in the hollowed-out bulbs that are at the base of the thorns. They feed on a sugary liquid that is found in the tree's leaves.

As the ants use the tree for shelter and food, the tree benefits, too. When another kind of animal starts grazing on the tree, the ants swarm and sting the animal, driving it away.

A colony of stinging ants makes its home in the swollen thorn acacia tree.

There is another example of interdependence that occurs in the Pacific Ocean. The sea anemone (uh NEHM uh nee) is an animal that lives on the ocean floor. It uses its poisonous tentacles to capture fish and other animals. But one type of fish is not in danger from the anemone. In fact, this fish makes its home right there among the tentacles.

Some scientists think that the clown fish has a coating on its body that protects it from the anemone's sting. In its home, the clown fish is safe from its own enemies. They stay away from the poisonous tentacles of the anemone. The anemone benefits from the clown fish, too. The fish keeps the anemone's tentacles clean by eating scraps of food that cling to them.

In Africa, a similar relationship exists between the Nile crocodile and a bird called the Egyptian plover. The crocodile allows the bird into its mouth. There the bird eats leeches attached to the crocodile's gums. Both animals benefit. The bird gets a meal. The crocodile gets its teeth cleaned.

MAIN IDEA **How are the clown fish and the sea anemone interdependent?**

◀ **The clown fish makes its home among the protective tentacles of the sea anemone.**

The Egyptian plover cleans the crocodile's teeth while getting a meal. ▶

Relationships in an Ecosystem

Every living thing has a role to play within its ecosystem. You can think of this as the particular job an organism does in its environment.

Plants play the role of producer (pruh DOO sur). A **producer** is an organism that makes its own food. The food that plants make is used for energy by organisms that eat the plants. All organisms need energy.

Plants use energy from sunlight to make food. In turn, plants use energy from the food they make to grow and to produce offspring. Some of the food is stored in the leaves, stems, and roots of a plant.

When an animal eats a plant, energy in the plant is transferred to the animal. Animals are consumers (kuhn SOO murz). A **consumer** gets energy by eating plants, or by eating other animals that eat plants. Consumers use this energy to live.

In the end, all the consumers in an ecosystem depend on producers for food. Without producers, the other organisms in an ecosystem could not survive.

A Rainforest Ecosystem

The kapok tree provides shelter for the macaws.

scarlet macaws

Trees are producers. Producers use the energy in sunlight to make food.

tapir

golden lion tamarin monkey

Animals are consumers. Consumers rely on producers, or other animals that eat producers, for food.

ferns

split-leaf plant

Shelter is another basic need of living things that is often met with the help of other organisms. For example, squirrels and many kinds of birds make their homes among the branches of trees. There, hidden in the leaves, the nests of these animals are protected from the hot sun. They are also protected from enemies.

Trees provide shelter and protection for plants, too. For example, some plants grow best in moist, shady conditions. Plants such as ferns and mosses might find shelter at the base of a tree.

Some animals provide shelter for other animals. Woodchucks make their homes by digging tunnels deep under the soil. But they are not the only ones that live in these tunnels. When the woodchuck moves on, animals such as skunks and rabbits may move in.

Hermit crabs also find shelter in homes built by other animals. Hermit crabs do not have a hard shell of their own. They use the shells that snails or other animals have left behind for shelter.

▶ **MAIN IDEA** **What is the relationship between producers and consumers?**

Pollinators and Seed Dispersal

In an ecosystem, some living things help other living things carry out reproduction (ree pruh DUHK-shuhn). **Reproduction** is the process of making more of one's own kind. It is another basic need of living things.

Many plants reproduce by making seeds. For a plant to make seeds, pollen (PAHL uhn) must be moved from one part of a flower to another, or from one flower to another. How does pollen move? Wind and water can carry pollen, but so can animals such as insects or birds. An animal that helps plants make seeds is called a **pollinator** (PAHL uh nay tur).

Pollinators feed on the pollen and nectar they find on flowers. As they feed, they carry pollen from flower to flower. When pollen touches the right part of the flower, seeds begin to form.

Some plants depend on animals to carry their seeds to new places where they can grow. **Seed dispersal** (dih SPUR suhl) is the scattering or carrying away of seeds from the plant that produced them. Some plant seeds get caught in the fur of animals. These seeds may be carried great distances from the parent plant before falling off and beginning to grow.

Some plants produce seeds that develop inside of fruit. Animals eat the fruit and either drop the seeds or deposit them in their waste. If conditions are favorable, the seeds will grow in their new location.

▶ **MAIN IDEA** How do plants depend on animals to reproduce?

Insects and birds help pollinate flowers and disperse seeds.

Visual Summary

Living things in an ecosystem are interdependent.

Consumers depend on producers for food.

Many plants depend on animals to help them reproduce and disperse seeds.

LINKS for Home and School

MATH Make a Diagram Imagine that the seeds of a certain plant cannot grow unless they are 2 meters away from the parent plant in any direction. Draw a diagram that shows where the seeds can grow and cannot grow.

SOCIAL STUDIES Classify Producers and Consumers People as well as animals are producers and consumers. As producers, people make goods or provide services. As consumers, they buy those goods or services. Interview some adults about what they produce and what they consume. Write a paragraph about your results.

Review

1 MAIN IDEA Name two ways that an animal might depend on a plant.

2 VOCABULARY Use the terms *producer* and *consumer* in a sentence.

3 READING SKILL: Main Idea and Details What main idea is illustrated by the interaction of the clown fish and the sea anemone?

4 CRITICAL THINKING: Apply Name one example of interdependence among animals in your local ecosystem.

5 INQUIRY SKILL: Analyze Data Classify each living thing shown in this lesson. Make a chart of your findings. Tell how many of each type are producers and how many are consumers.

 TEST PREP

All animals in an ecosystem depend on ___.

A. producers

B. consumers

C. pollinators

D. seeds

 Technology
Visit **www.eduplace.com/scp/** to do more research on interdependence.

The Vanishing MANATEE

Manatees are definitely extreme. As a species, they are extremely old. Florida fossils show they've been part of Florida's ecosystem since prehistoric times. They are also extremely heavy. An average adult is ten feet long and can weigh over 3,500 pounds —as much as a car!

Unfortunately, the manatee is also extremely *rare*—and probably endangered. No one knows how many Florida manatees are left, but a fair guess is just two to three thousand. Their numbers have been drastically reduced by human activities, but many Floridians are working hard to protect the manatee and its environment.

Extremely cute
What a face! Everybody loves a manatee. For all their extreme bulk, they are completely harmless, and even beneficial.

Extremely slow

Manatees spend so much time floating on the surface that algae literally grows on their backs!

Be Careful!

These workers are giving first aid to a manatee wounded by a boat propeller. Because manatees like to float and sleep on the surface, many of them are injured or killed by powerboats. Most manatees you see in the wild have propeller scars.

Vocabulary

Complete each sentence with a term from the list.

1. All the members of one kind of plant or animal living together in one area are known as a/an _____.

2. The wind carrying dandelion seeds is an example of _____.

3. The loose material in which most plants grow is called _____.

4. All the living things in an ecosystem make up a/an _____.

5. An organism that makes its own food is a/an _____.

6. Material that is rich in nutrients and comes from the remains of plants and animals is called _____.

7. A grassy land area with very few trees is called a/an _____.

8. All the living and nonliving things in an area make up a/an _____.

9. An animal that gets energy by eating plants or by eating other animals that eat plants is a/an _____.

10. An animal that carries pollen from flower to flower is a/an _____.

community B12
consumer B24
ecosystem B6
environment B12
organic matter B6
pollinator B26
population B12
prairie B14
producer B24
rainforest B14
reproduction B26
seed dispersal B26
soil B6
temperate zone B15

Test Prep

Write the letter of the best answer choice.

11. An area on Earth where the temperature is rarely very hot or very cold is called a/an _____.

    A. prairie.   C. temperate zone.
    B. environment.   D. rainforest.

12. Everything that surrounds and affects a living thing is called its _____.

    A. environment.   C. population.
    B. temperate zone.   D. ecosystem.

13. The process of making more of one's own kind is called _____.

    A. population.   C. pollinator.
    B. reproduction.   D. community.

14. Which of the following areas gets a lot of rainfall?

    A. rainforest   C. desert
    B. temperate zone   D. prairie

Inquiry Skills

15. **Observe** Imagine that you are an explorer traveling in a desert ecosystem. What conditions are you likely to observe on your journey?

16. **Classify** Trillium plants, pine trees, owls, and deer can all be found in a forest ecosystem. Which of these are producers and which are consumers?

Map the Concept

Use terms from the following list to complete the concept map.

consumers
sunlight
temperature
air
soil
producers
water

Nonliving Parts of an Ecosystem	Living Parts of an Ecosystem
_____	_____
_____	_____
_____	_____
_____	_____

Critical Thinking

17. **Apply** What might happen to a population of flowering plants if all the pollinators in the ecosystem disappeared?

18. **Synthesize** Identify some of the nonliving things in an ocean ecosystem. Then describe some of the conditions in an ocean ecosystem.

19. **Evaluate** What might you say to someone who told you that soil is not an important part of an ecosystem?

20. **Analyze** Explain the difference between an ecosystem and a community.

Performance Assessment

Build an Ecosystem
Imagine that you can create your own ecosystem. What would the nonliving conditions (sunlight, temperature, rainfall) be? What living and nonliving things would be found in the ecosystem? How would the living things interact with the nonliving conditions? How would the living things interact with one another? Make a drawing of your ecosystem. Label all the living and nonliving things.

Chapter 6

Matter and Energy in Ecosystems

LESSON 1

Energy from a star that is millions of kilometers away reaches Earth—how is this energy transformed into the food that most living things need to survive?

Read about it in Lesson 1.

LESSON 2

An old piece of bread and a decaying log—what kinds of organisms use these as sources of food?

Read about it in Lesson 2.

How Does Energy Flow in a Food Web?

Why It Matters...

When you run, your body uses energy. Your body also uses energy when you sit perfectly still and read. Just breathing takes energy. Like you, other animals need energy to survive. A hawk needs energy to fly. A fish needs energy to swim. Living things get their energy from food.

PREPARE TO INVESTIGATE

Inquiry Skill

Use Models You can use a model of an object, process, or idea to better understand or describe how it works.

Materials

- Food Web Resource
- reference books
- 4 index cards
- construction paper
- markers or crayons
- scissors

A Tangled Web

Procedure

1 **Research** Work with a partner. Use a reference book. From the list provided, find a plant-eating animal. In your *Science Notebook*, record that animal and the plants it eats. Then research and record an animal from the list that eats the plant eater. Next, find a new animal that eats that one.

2 On separate index cards, draw and label each living thing from step 1.

3 **Use Models** Place the index cards in order on construction paper to show a food chain. A **food chain** (chayn) shows how organisms get food, or energy. Draw arrows to show how energy flows from one living thing to another.

4 **Collaborate** Turn over your construction paper. Work with another team. Use cards from both teams to make a food web. A **food web** is two or more interconnected food chains. Draw arrows to show how energy flows.

Conclusion

1. **Infer** Does energy flow from plant eaters to animal eaters or from animal eaters to plant eaters? How do you know?

2. **Predict** What might happen if one kind of animal is removed from the web?

STEP 1

STEP 3

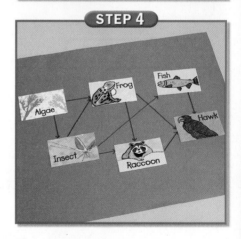

STEP 4

Investigate More!

Research Use the Internet or talk to an expert to find out what animals live near your school. Create a food web to show how energy flows from one to another.

B35

Path of Energy

READING SKILL

Sequence Use a chart to show the transfer of energy from the Sun to a carnivore.

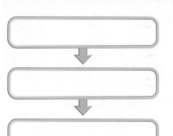

MAIN IDEA In an ecosystem, energy flows from the Sun to producers and then from producers to consumers.

Energy from the Sun

All living things need energy to survive. They get that energy from food. You know that some animals eat plants and some animals eat other animals that eat plants.

Plants do not eat food. Most plants make their own food through a process called **photosynthesis** (foh toh SIHN thih sihs). Photosynthesis takes place in a plant's leaves. A material in the leaves traps light energy from the Sun. During photosynthesis, plants use carbon dioxide gas from the air to make food in the form of sugar. The original source of energy for most living things is the Sun.

Almost all organisms on Earth get energy from the Sun.

Sun

plant

Predator and Prey

An animal that hunts other animals for food is called a **predator** (PREHD uh tawr). A fox is one kind of predator. A rabbit is prey (pray) for a fox. A **prey** is an animal that is hunted for food by another animal. An animal can be both predator and prey. For example, a fox may be the prey of a bobcat.

The illustration shows how energy flows from the Sun to plants. Recall that plants are producers and animals are consumers. When a consumer, such as a rabbit, eats a plant, it receives some of the plant's energy. When the rabbit becomes the prey of the fox, the fox receives a smaller amount of the plant's energy.

In a pond ecosystem, tiny plants are the producers. They use the Sun's energy to make food. Tiny animals eat the plants. The tiny animals are prey to small fish. The small fish are eaten by larger fish.

In each case, energy flows from the Sun to a producer, and then to consumers. Among the consumers, energy flows from prey to predator. When tiny animals in the pond eat the tiny plants, the energy flows to them. When predators eat the tiny animals, the energy transfers to them.

▶ **SEQUENCE** **What is the relationship between a predator and its prey?**

prey

predator

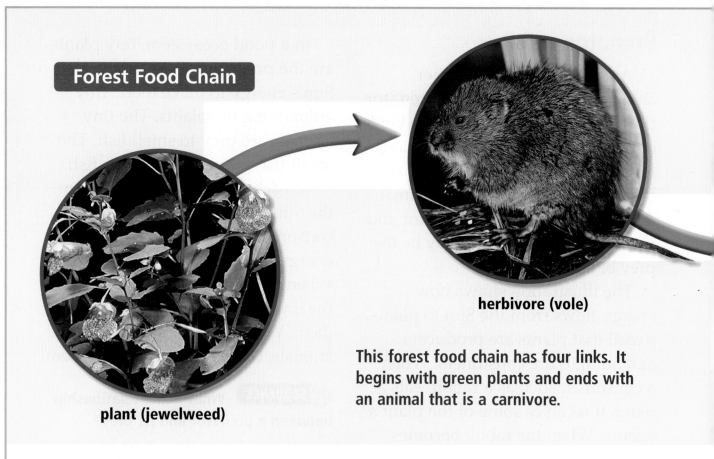

Forest Food Chain

plant (jewelweed)

herbivore (vole)

This forest food chain has four links. It begins with green plants and ends with an animal that is a carnivore.

Food Chains

A **food chain** shows the path of food energy in an ecosystem from plants to animals. In the food chain shown, a vole gets energy from eating a plant called jewelweed. The skunk gets energy from eating the vole. The owl gets energy from eating the skunk.

Food chains are different in different ecosystems. But the first link in a food chain is always a producer. In most ecosystems, the producers are green plants. Matter and energy enter the food chain through these plants. This happens when the plants, such as the jewelweed, use the energy in

sunlight to make food through the process of photosynthesis.

The second link in the food chain shown is a vole. A vole is an herbivore (HUR buh vawr). An **herbivore** is an animal that eats only plants. The vole gets energy from the green plants it eats.

The third and fourth links in any food chain are either carnivores (KAHR nuh vawrz) or omnivores (AHM nuh vawrz). An **omnivore** is an animal that eats both plants and animals. A skunk is an omnivore. It eats insects, earthworms, mice, and voles. It also eats berries and nuts.

A **carnivore** is an animal that eats only other animals. The great

omnivore (skunk)

carnivore (owl)

horned owl is a carnivore. The owl gets energy by eating the skunk.

In a pond ecosystem, the tiny plants are the first link in the food chain. The tiny animals that eat the tiny plants are the second link in the chain. Recall that plant-eating organisms are herbivores. Other links in a pond food chain are the small and large fish that eat the herbivores.

A raccoon is an omnivore that is often a part of a pond ecosystem. A raccoon eats the small fish in the chain. Because it is an omnivore, it also eats plant material such as berries and acorns.

At each link in a food chain, some of the food energy is lost. For example, a sunflower plant does not store all the food that it makes. Some of the energy from the food is used to develop flowers and seeds for the plant.

A deer that eats the sunflower gets only some of the energy the plant captured from the Sun. The deer uses some of the energy from the sunflower to run from predators. So less energy is available to a predator that eats the deer. In a food chain, the further the link is from producers, the less energy there is available. Because of this, most food chains have only four or five links.

▶ **SEQUENCE** **What are the third and fourth links in a food chain?**

Food Webs

Most ecosystems contain many different kinds of plants and animals. Each plant or animal is part of more than one food chain. When two or more food chains overlap, they form a **food web**. In a food web, at least one plant or animal from each food chain is part of another food chain.

For example, the clover, grasshopper, woodpecker, and owl form a food chain. They are also part of a food web. In the food web shown, the grasshopper is not only prey for the woodpecker. It is prey for the snake, too. The grasshopper is part of a second food chain that contains the snake. The snake and woodpecker may compete with each other for this food resource.

▶ **MAIN IDEA** What makes up a food web?

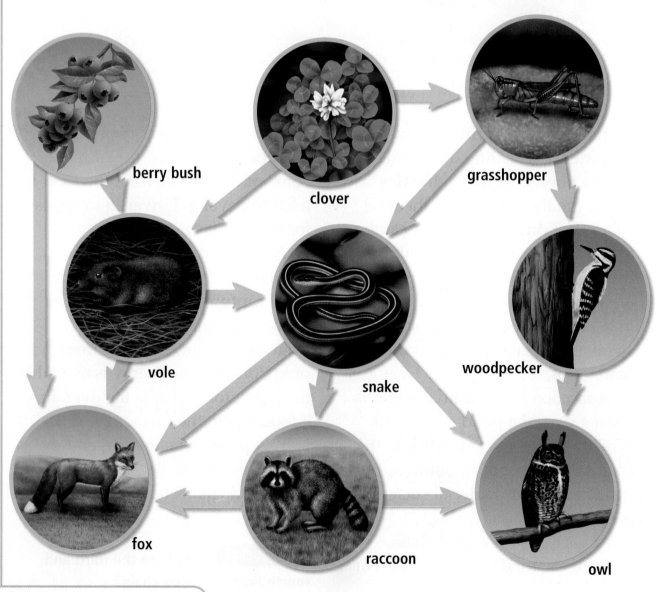

berry bush

clover

grasshopper

vole

snake

woodpecker

fox

raccoon

owl

Visual Summary

Almost all living things on Earth get energy from the Sun.

Food chains show how food energy flows through an ecosystem.

Two or more food chains connect to form a food web.

LINKS for Home and School

MATH **Make a Graph** These are the wingspans of some birds of prey: American Kestrel, 21 inches; Barn Owl, 44 inches; Red-Tailed Hawk, 52 inches, and Bald Eagle, 80 inches. Make a bar graph to compare them.

LITERATURE **Make a Drawing** Read more about food chains in *Food Chain Frenzy* (*Magic School Bus* Chapter Book, 17) by Anne Capeci, John Speirs, and Joanna Cole. To draw a food web, find an animal that would connect to one of the food chains in the book.

Review

1 MAIN IDEA Describe the flow of energy in a food web.

2 VOCABULARY Compare and contrast food chains and food webs.

3 READING SKILL: Sequence Explain how the energy plants make during photosynthesis is passed to predators.

4 CRITICAL THINKING: Apply Are human beings herbivores, carnivores, or omnivores? What evidence supports your answer?

5 INQUIRY SKILL: Use Models Draw a food chain that includes yourself.

TEST PREP An animal that is eaten by another animal is a(n) ___.

A. predator

B. prey

C. carnivore

D. omnivore

 Technology Visit **www.eduplace.com/scp/** to learn more about food webs.

Rachel Carson
1907–1964

Rachel Carson's life-long love of science and nature led her to publish works that encouraged others to protect the environment. As a girl, Carson spent hours exploring the outdoors. She loved writing as much as she loved nature. She published her first article in a children's magazine at the age of 10.

In 1962, Carson published *Silent Spring*, a best-seller that is still in print. Carson had observed that birds were dying from pesticides (PEHS tih sydz). Pesticides are poisonous chemicals that are sprayed on crops to kill insects.

Carson realized that if birds were in danger, the food web they were part of might be suffering. She spent four years researching information on the damage pesticides do to Earth's wildlife and the environment. The result of her research, *Silent Spring,* is regarded as the inspiration of the modern environmental movement.

SILENT
SPRING
40TH ANNIVERSARY EDITION
RACHEL
CARSON

Rachel Carson believed that people had the power to help or harm the natural world. *Silent Spring* and her other books taught people the importance of protecting Earth's land, water, and air.

Sharing Ideas

1. **READING CHECK** What observations first led Rachel Carson to write *Silent Spring*?

2. **WRITE ABOUT IT** What effect did *Silent Spring* have?

3. **TALK ABOUT IT** Discuss the importance of protecting the environment.

B43

How Is Matter Cycled in an Ecosystem?

Why It Matters...

Nothing in nature goes to waste. A vulture will make a meal of the remains of an animal killed by a predator. Perhaps you have thrown away bread because there was mold growing on it. For humans, the moldy bread is waste. For the mold, it is a source of food!

PREPARE TO INVESTIGATE

Inquiry Skill

Use Variables A variable is the condition that is being tested in an experiment. All conditions in an experiment must be kept the same, except for the variable.

Materials

- marking pen
- 3 resealable plastic bags
- 3 pieces of bread
- dropper
- water
- masking tape
- black construction paper

Growing Mold
Procedure

1. **Collaborate** Work with a partner. Use a marking pen to label three plastic bags A, B, and C. In your *Science Notebook*, make a chart like the one shown.

2. **Experiment** Put a piece of bread into each bag. Use a dropper to put 10 drops of water on the bread in each bag. Seal the bags and tape them closed with masking tape. **Safety:** Do not open any of the bags after sealing. Your teacher will dispose of them.

3. **Observe** Record in your chart the appearance of the bread in each bag.

4. **Use Variables** Place bag *A* in a refrigerator and bag *B* in a dark closet. Use a sheet of black construction paper to cover bag *C*. Place it in a sunny window. Temperature is the variable you are testing.

5. **Record Data** Observe each bag every day for about two weeks. In your chart, record any changes. Look for the growth of mold, a type of organism. Draw what you see.

Conclusion

1. **Analyze Data** How was the growth of mold different in the three bags?

2. **Infer** Under which condition did the mold grow best?

STEP 1

Appearance of Bread

Day	Bag A (cold)	Bag B (room temp)	Bag C (warm)
1			
2			
3			
4			
5			

STEP 2

Investigate More!

Design an Experiment
How might light affect the growth of bread mold? Using the same materials, plan an experiment to find out. Make sure you set up all the bags in the same way except for the variable of light. Share your plan with your teacher.

VOCABULARY

decay	p. B48
decomposer	p. B48
microorganism	p. B49
recycling	p. B48
scavenger	p. B46

READING SKILL

Cause and Effect As you read, write down the effect that scavengers and decomposers have on ecosystems.

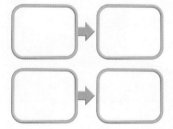

Recycling Matter in Ecosystems

MAIN IDEA Some organisms get food energy by eating the remains of dead organisms. These organisms are an important part of an ecosystem.

Scavengers

Have you ever gone on a scavenger (SKAV-uhn jur) hunt? If so, you know that it involves looking for things that exist in the environment. Some animals spend much of their time "on a scavenger hunt." Unlike predators, they are not hunting for living prey. They are looking for the remains of dead animals to eat. A **scavenger** is an animal that feeds on the remains or wastes of other animals.

Scavengers are consumers. Like all consumers, they get energy from the food they eat. For a scavenger, the energy comes from eating the remains of once-living things. Often a scavenger eats the remains of prey that was killed by another animal. Raccoons, vultures, hyenas, and some crabs are scavengers.

Carrion beetles lay their eggs in the remains of animals. The flesh of the animal provides food for the developing young. ▶

Predators and Scavengers

Predators and scavengers are both carnivores. Predators hunt and kill other animals for food. Scavengers eat what is left by the predators. For example, when a wolf kills a moose for food, it does not eat all of the moose. The leftovers provide hearty meals for coyotes, ravens, and other scavengers.

Scavengers take in nutrients that would otherwise be wasted. If the scavenger becomes the prey of another animal, the nutrients are passed along in the food chain. This is one reason why scavengers are an important part of a food web.

Scavengers are a part of every kind of ecosystem. In the ocean, sharks and crabs are scavengers. Although sharks hunt live prey, they also eat organisms that are no longer alive.

▶ **CAUSE AND EFFECT** Why are scavengers an important part of food webs?

▲ Peccaries are both omnivores and scavengers. They will eat almost anything, including meat, fruit, fish, and birds.

In Africa, Marabou (MAIR uh-boo) storks are commonly seen in garbage dumps. They are both carnivores and scavengers. ▶

Helpful Organisms

Fungi (FUHN jy) are a variety of organisms that include mushrooms and mold. Mold can cause foods to spoil. Other kinds of fungi can cause disease. Bacteria (bak TIHR-ee uh) are tiny one-celled organisms that are found in all environments and in all living things. Some types of bacteria can cause disease.

However, most fungi and bacteria are helpful. They have an important role as decomposers (dee kuhm POH zurz).

All organisms die. You already know that some dead organisms are eaten by scavengers. But some are not. Instead, after death, their bodies **decay** (dih KAY), or break down into simpler materials. Decomposers help this process. A **decomposer** is a living thing that breaks down the remains of dead organisms. All food chains end with decomposers. A fallen tree, or log, is a good place to find decomposers. Decomposers found there include worms, fungi, bacteria, and insects such as termites.

By helping the wood decay, decomposers help new plants grow. Nutrients that were in the wood are released back into the soil by decomposers. This **recycling** (ree SY-kuhl ihng), or process of breaking down materials into a different form that can be used again, is important to an ecosystem.

A Home for Many Living Things

This log has decomposers, scavengers, producers, herbivores, and carnivores living on it.

beetle

oyster fungus

ant

salamander

Decay happens much faster in warm, moist conditions than in cold, dry conditions. An animal that died atop a cold mountain might not decay for a long time. If that same animal died in a warm, rainy area, the body would decay rapidly!

Decomposers help the environment. They keep it from becoming crowded with the remains of dead plants and animals. They also recycle valuable nutrients. Much of this "cleaning" and recycling is done by decomposers called microorganisms (my-kroh AWR guh nihz uhmz). A **microorganism** is a tiny living thing that can only be seen with the aid of a microscope. Bacteria are one type of microorganism.

As you've learned, bacteria help in the decay of dead plants and animals. Nutrients released from these remains enrich the soil. Many kinds of plants in an ecosystem benefit from this enriched soil.

Another type of helpful microorganism is a fungi that is found on the roots of some plants. These fungi grow out into the soil and act like a second root system. They absorb minerals and water from the soil that the plant can then use. Plants that have fungi on their roots are better able to survive than those that do not.

▶ **CAUSE AND EFFECT** **What is one way that decomposers are helpful?**

mouse

fern

moss

termites

millipede

Benefits to Plants and Animals

Decomposers are a very important part of ecosystems. They release nutrients that plants and animals need to survive. The nutrients are released into the soil and water. Nutrients in the soil help plants stay healthy.

Decomposers free up living space in the environment. When the remains of dead plants and animals decay, the space they took up becomes available to other living things.

Because decomposers are helpful, it makes sense to encourage their growth. People can create an ideal environment for decomposers by making a compost (KAHM pohst) pile. A compost pile or compost bin is a place that is set aside for the decay of materials that were part of once-living things. Many materials that can be put in a compost pile are often thrown in the trash. When these materials end up in a landfill, they take up space and may not decay very much.

Materials that should be put in compost piles include grass clippings, leaves, kitchen scraps, and some papers. These materials are recycled by decomposers such as fungi and bacteria that live in great numbers in a compost pile. The resulting decayed material can be mixed with soil. The enriched soil that results can be used to grow plants for food.

▶ **CAUSE AND EFFECT** **How can compost improve soil?**

◀ Backyard compost pile

Food, yard waste, paper, and cardboard could all be composted. What percent of all the garbage is that? ▼

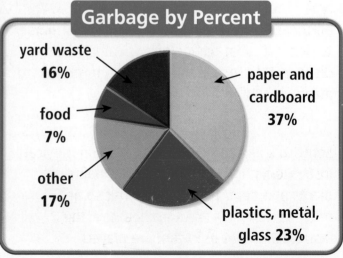

Garbage by Percent

yard waste 16%

food 7%

other 17%

paper and cardboard 37%

plastics, metal, glass 23%

Lesson Wrap-Up

Visual Summary

Scavengers get energy from the remains of dead organisms.

Decomposers help decay, or break down, the remains of dead organisms.

The process of recycling nutrients and other materials from organic matter is important to every ecosystem.

LINKS for Home and School

TECHNOLOGY Measuring an Organism The world's largest organism, a type of underground fungus, was found in northeastern Oregon. Use the Internet or library to find out what technology scientists used to discover that this was a single organism and to measure its size.

MUSIC Research Musical Instruments Some of the materials used in making musical instruments are made from the remains of plants and animals. Find out what some of these materials are. Describe how the instruments that use them are played.

Review

1. **MAIN IDEA** What two types of organisms get energy from the remains of once-living things?

2. **VOCABULARY** Use the term *microorganism* in a sentence.

3. **READING SKILL: Cause and Effect** Explain two ways that a population of scavengers would be affected if all the predators in an area were to disappear.

4. **CRITICAL THINKING: Infer** What would be the effect on an ecosystem if there were no decomposers?

5. **INQUIRY SKILL: Use Variables** In an experiment, one decaying log is placed in a covered cardboard box and another in a clear box. The temperature and amount of water for each are the same. What is the variable being tested?

✓ **TEST PREP**
A living thing that breaks down the remains of dead organisms is a ___.

A. prey

B. decomposer

C. predator

D. carnivore

Technology
Visit **www.eduplace.com/scp/** to investigate more about scavengers and decomposers.

B51

Extreme Science

Nothing Wasted!

Hey, what's this beetle pushing around? Don't laugh, but it's a big ball of animal dung. The beetle has carefully rolled up the dung to make it into a nursery for its baby. Dung beetles also eat dung. They are among the most important scavengers on Earth. Without them, the dung of plant-eating animals would overwhelm some ecosystems.

Elephants eat plants and drop dung.

Beetle rolls up ball of dung.

The Dung Beetle Cycle

Buried dung ball fertilizes plants.

New beetle hatches from dung ball.

Beetle buries dung ball with egg inside.

▼ These amazing beetles roll up and bury most of the thousands of tons of dung dropped by plant-eaters in the Serengeti of Africa.

Vocabulary

Complete each sentence with a term from the list.

1. Most plants make food through the process of _____.

2. A rabbit is _____ for a fox.

3. A tiny organism that cannot be seen without a microscope is a/an _____.

4. An animal that gets energy by eating the remains or wastes of other organisms is called a/an _____.

5. An organism that helps a dead tree break down into simpler materials is called a/an _____.

6. An animal that eats both plants and animals is a/an _____.

7. The path of energy in an ecosystem as one living thing eats another is shown by a/an _____.

8. Two or more overlapping food chains form a/an _____.

9. The breakdown of the remains of a dead organism into simpler materials is called _____.

10. An animal that hunts other animals for food is a/an _____.

carnivore B38
decay B48
decomposer B48
food chain B38
food web B40
herbivore B38
microorganism B49
omnivore B38
photosynthesis B36
predator B37
prey B37
recycling B48
scavenger B46

 Test Prep

Write the letter of the best answer choice.

11. Which of the following is an animal that eats only other animals?

   A. carnivore   **C.** herbivore
   B. a scavenger   **D.** omnivore

12. Which of the following is an animal that eats only plants?

   A. carnivore   **C.** herbivore
   B. scavenger   **D.** omnivore

13. The release of nutrients from a rotting log back into the soil is an example of _____.

   A. consuming.   **C.** photosynthesis.
   B. recycling.   **D.** food energy.

14. All food chains end with _____.

   A. producers.   **C.** decomposers.
   B. scavengers.   **D.** herbivores.

15. **Use Models** Draw a food web that includes at least six organisms. Label each organism to show its role in the food web.

16. **Use Variables** Shanika wants to run a two-week test on the effect of different amounts of light on water plants. She has three test tubes. Into each test tube she puts water and a chemical that changes color when oxygen is present. She puts a water plant into each test tube. Where should she place each test tube for the next two weeks?

Map the Concept

The concept map shows the flow of energy in ecosystems. Write each term in the correct place on the map.

herbivores
decomposers
producers
carnivores

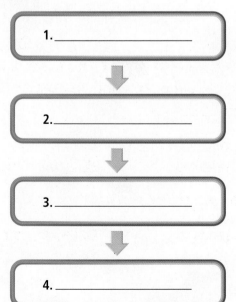

1. _____

2. _____

3. _____

4. _____

17. **Apply** Your friend tells you that she is a vegetarian and does not eat meat or any animal products. What kind of consumer is your friend? Explain.

18. **Synthesize** If humans caught all of the tuna fish in an ocean ecosystem, how might that ecosystem be affected?

19. **Evaluate** Think about the following statement: Herbivores and carnivores are more important to a food web than are omnivores. Is this statement accurate? Why or why not? Use examples in your explanation.

20. **Analyze** How is decay helpful in an ecosystem? Explain.

Performance Assessment

Parts of a Food Chain

What food chains might exist in a city park? Draw a diagram of a food chain in a city park that includes plants and animals. Compare your diagram with those of other students. Evaluate whether any of the food chains form a food web.

Chapter **7**

Adaptation and Extinction

LESSON

1

Jackrabbits have very large ears—how does this help them survive in the desert?

Read about it in Lesson 1.

LESSON

2

Overhunting and the building of a dam— how might each threaten the survival of plants and animals?

Read about it in Lesson 2.

LESSON

3

Pterosaurs were flying reptiles that died out 65 million years ago— how do scientists study them today?

Read about it in Lesson 3.

How Are Organisms Adapted to Survive?

Why It Matters...

You may think the picture on this page shows a plant. In fact, you are looking at an animal. The lettuce sea slug hides from enemies by blending in with its surroundings. Many animals have colors or shapes that help them survive.

PREPARE TO INVESTIGATE

Inquiry Skill

Observe When you observe, you gather information about the environment using your five senses: seeing, hearing, smelling, touching, and tasting.

Materials

- black construction paper
- plastic jars
- scissors
- masking tape
- small index card
- mealworms
- clock or watch

Science and Math Toolbox

For step 5, review **Measuring Elapsed Time** on page H12.

A Mealworm Home
Procedure

1. **Collaborate** Work with a partner. Use black construction paper to cover the outside of a plastic jar as shown.

STEP 1

2. Cut a square of black paper that is slightly larger than the opening of the jar. Position the square over the opening of the jar. Leaving a space, tape the square in place as shown.

STEP 2

3. Use an index card to lift a mealworm and place it in an uncovered plastic jar. **Safety:** Handle the mealworms gently.

4. **Observe** With your partner, use masking tape to join together the openings of the two jars. Place the joined jars on their side in a well-lit area.

STEP 3

5. **Record Data** Every 10 minutes for the next half hour, observe and record the location of the mealworm. When you are finished, have your teacher return the mealworm to a suitable environment.

Conclusion

1. **Predict** Suppose in step 4 you put the mealworm home in a dark place. How do you think this would affect the mealworm's movements?

2. **Infer** Based on your observations, what can you conclude about the type of environment a mealworm prefers?

Investigate More!
Design an Experiment
How would the mealworm move if it was placed in the covered jar first? Plan an experiment to find out. Then get your teacher's permission to carry it out.

VOCABULARY

adaptation	p. B60
camouflage	p. B62
habitat	p. B60
hibernate	p. B64
mimicry	p. B63
niche	p. B60

READING SKILL

Problem-Solution
Use a chart to show how a plant or animal adaptation solves a problem.

Problem	Solution

Adaptations For Survival

MAIN IDEA To survive, plants and animals must be adapted to their environment. Their adaptations help organisms obtain food, hide from other animals, and generally survive the conditions of their environment.

Plant and Animal Adaptations

Sharks live in water, and cactuses grow in dry deserts. It's clear that different plants and animals survive in different environments. The place where a plant or animal lives is called its **habitat** (HAB ih tat). The ocean is a dolphin's habitat. The habitat of a toucan is the rainforest.

Plants and animals have adaptations (ad-ap TAY shuhnz) that help them survive. An **adaptation** can be a physical feature or a behavior that helps a plant or animal survive.

The role a plant or animal plays in its environment is called its **niche** (nihch). A niche includes the kind of food an organism uses for energy. It also includes the conditions the organism needs to survive. Part of an opossum's niche is to eat berries. Many organisms can share a habitat, but each organism has its own niche.

▶ **PROBLEM AND SOLUTION** Give an example of how an animal adaptation solves a problem.

A wood duck's feet have sharp claws that help it perch on branches. Its feet are also webbed to help it swim.

Adaptations to Habitat

Forest
The aye aye has large eyes that help it see at night. The aye aye's third finger is very long and thin. It uses it for digging food out of trees.

Rain Forest
Water that stays on leaves can cause disease. The leaves of many rainforest plants have pointed ends that allow rainwater to drip off.

Desert
Light-colored fur helps the jackrabbit blend into its surroundings. Its large ears help it keep cool in the desert by giving off heat.

Tundra
The musk ox's habitat is covered with snow much of the year. How might the musk ox's thick fur help it survive?

Camouflage

Have you ever seen an animal that looked so much like its surroundings that you almost didn't notice it? Such an animal has an adaptation called camouflage (KAM uh flahzh). **Camouflage** is the coloring, marking, or other physical appearance of an animal that helps it blend in with its surroundings.

Animals use camouflage to hide from both predators and prey. The camouflage of the lettuce sea slug on page B58 helps it hide from ocean predators. The color and pattern of the young deer's fur helps the deer blend in with its forest habitat. The young deer is protected because predators have a hard time seeing it.

A Bengal tiger is a predator that uses camouflage. Its stripes help the tiger blend with the tall grass where it hunts at dawn and dusk. Its prey does not see the tiger approach.

Some animals change color as their environment changes. For example, the fur of an arctic fox's coat is gray in the summer, so the fox blends with the rocky ground. In winter, the fox's coat turns white. This white coat helps the fox blend in with its snow-covered surroundings. The arctic fox can hunt without being seen.

The white fur of the arctic fox helps camouflage it in snow. ▶

◄ A young deer's light-brown fur and white spots look like patches of sunlight and shade.

Color and Mimicry

Some animals have bright colors that let other animals see them easily. This adaptation is called warning coloration. The bright colors of a bumble bee can warn of painful stings. The blue poison dart frog stands out in its habitat. The frog's bright color warns predators that it is poisonous.

Some animals protect themselves by using mimicry (MIHM ih kree). **Mimicry** is an adaptaton that allows an animal to protect itself by looking like another kind of animal or like a plant. Many insects use mimicry. The South American owl butterfly has large spots on its wings that look like the eyes of an owl. These spots scare away birds that might want to eat the butterfly.

Mimicry is also useful to animals that hunt. By looking like an animal that is not a threat, a predator can fool its prey. For example, a leafy sea dragon looks like a floating clump of seaweed. Small sea animals are not afraid to get close to this "seaweed." When they do, the leafy sea dragon catches them with its tube-shaped mouth.

▶ **PROBLEM AND SOLUTION** How does mimicry help an animal survive?

◀ The South American owl butterfly uses mimicry to scare away birds.

The bright color of the blue poison dart frog makes the frog easy to see and warns predators to stay away. ▶

Behavior

Behavior, as well as appearance, can help a predator as it hunts its prey. Humpback whales blow circles of bubbles around schools of fish. The fish cannot escape from the circle and become easy prey for the whales. Wolves and other animals hunt in groups. The group surrounds the prey so it cannot easily escape.

Behavior also helps prey survive. Rabbits run in a zig-zag pattern, which helps them dodge predators. Zebras use their hooves and teeth to defend themselves.

In some environments, winter brings freezing temperatures and snow. Animals such as bats, frogs, and chipmunks have an adaptation that helps them survive the cold winter. They **hibernate** (HY bur-nayt), or go into a deep sleep, during which they use very little energy and usually do not need to eat. In this deep sleep, the animal's heartbeat and breathing rate slow down.

▶ **PROBLEM AND SOLUTION** What are two examples of adaptations that help animals hunt?

▲ The kangaroo rat survives in the desert by staying in its burrow during the heat of the day.

◀ This archer fish catches insects by shooting them down with a strong jet of water.

Visual Summary

Camouflage helps animals blend into their surroundings.

Mimicry helps animals protect themselves by looking like other things.

Adaptations

Some animals hibernate to survive winter cold.

Hunting in groups helps some animals.

for Home and School

TECHNOLOGY Make Comparisons

Many human inventions are modeled on animal adaptations. Research the snowshoe hare and the shovel-nosed snake. Describe inventions that are similar to adaptations of these animals. Tell how the invention is similar in its form and function to the adaptation.

WRITING Story

Select an animal you have read about in this lesson or elsewhere. The animal should have an unusual or interesting adaptation. Write a short children's story about the animal. You might wish to make it an adventure story that could be read to a child.

Review

❶ MAIN IDEA Explain why it is important for plants and animals to be adapted to their environment.

❷ VOCABULARY What is camouflage?

❸ READING SKILL: Problem-Solution How does hibernation help frogs survive the winter?

❹ CRITICAL THINKING: Apply Some katydids (KAY tee dihds) look like the leaves they live on. What might happen to a katydid in the fall when the leaves change color?

❺ INQUIRY SKILL: Observe What features of an insect would you look at to determine what adaptations the insect has?

 TEST PREP

Hawks are birds that hunt small animals. A hawk would most likely have feet with ___.

A. webs

B. large claws

C. small toes

D. no claws

 Technology

Visit **www.eduplace.com/scp/** to find out more about adaptations for survival.

What Threatens the Survival of Species?

Why It Matters...

The giant panda eats only bamboo. To survive, it needs to eat large amounts. People have cut down bamboo to use the land for other purposes. Because there is less bamboo, the survival of pandas is in danger.

PREPARE TO INVESTIGATE

Inquiry Skill

Compare When you compare two things, you observe how they are alike and how they are different.

Materials

- 3 plastic containers of pond water, labeled A, B, and C
- flashlight

Science and Math Toolbox

For step 1, review **Making a Chart to Organize Data** on page H10.

Algae Growth
Procedure

1. **Collaborate** Work with a partner. In your *Science Notebook*, make a chart like the one shown.

2. **Observe** Shine a flashlight through the side of each of three containers of pond water. Record your observations in the chart.

3. **Infer** Two of the containers have different amounts of plant food mixed with the pond water. One contains no plant food. Infer which jar contains a small amount of plant food, which contains a large amount of plant food, and which contains no plant food. Based on your observations in step 2, make an inference about which container has the most plant food.

4. **Observe** Put the containers in a sunny window for four days. Then repeat steps 2 and 3.

5. **Communicate** Write a brief paragraph in your *Science Notebook* explaining how you made your inferences.

Conclusion

1. **Predict** What effect do you think adding plant food would have on algae growth in a small pond?

2. **Hypothesize** In what way could adding plant food to a small pond be a threat to the survival of other organisms in the pond?

STEP 1

Container	A	B	C
Observations at start			
Inferences			
Observations after 4 days			
Inferences			

STEP 2

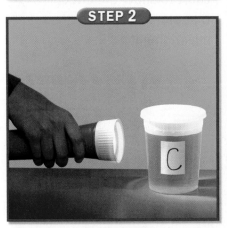

STEP 3

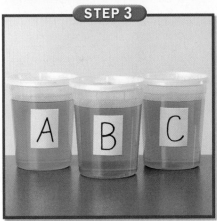

Investigate More!
Solve a Problem
You notice that the water in a pond suddenly looks cloudy. Working as a team, make a plan to find out what caused it and what to do about it.

VOCABULARY

species	p. B70
extinct	p. B70
migrate	p. B70

READING SKILL

Cause and Effect Use a chart to show the effect that animals have on their environment.

Threats to Survival

MAIN IDEA Different species of plants and animals face a number of threats to their survival.

How Organisms Change Environments

Swarms of South American leaf-cutter ants march to a tree. Each ant cuts a large piece of a leaf and carries it back to the nest. The leaves are used by the insects to grow fungi—their food source. In the process, an entire tree may lose all of its leaves and be destroyed. Organisms living in or on the tree have lost their home.

Whether it is an ant, a plant, or a human, every living thing causes changes in its environment. And these changes affect other living things.

Sometimes a change that is harmful to one organism is helpful to another. Although leaf-cutter ants destroy certain green plants, they help fungi. They create ideal conditions for the growth of certain kinds of fungi. The leaves they cut are organic matter that the fungi use for food.

When leaf-cutter ants take all the leaves from a tree, the tree may die.

The Aswan Dam was built in 1970 to control floods that caused damage.

EGYPT

Nile River

Aswan dam

Lake Nasser

Area that used to flood

Sometimes, without any active behavior, an organism affects how another living thing meets its needs. For example, a maple tree seedling begins growing in a flowerbed. If allowed to grow, the maple tree will provide a home for many organisms. But that same tree may grow so large that it blocks the sunlight needed by the plants that once grew near it. Only plants that require less sunlight can now survive beneath the tree.

Humans can use technology to change a forest into a city or a river into a lake. These changes have good and bad effects. The Aswan Dam in Egypt has helped people in a number of ways. It was built to hold back the flood waters of the Nile River. The dam provides electricity. By making water flow steady, it has also improved travel on the river.

But the dam has done harm as well as good. Before the dam, flooding deposited soil rich in nutrients along the river's banks. Without this rich soil, farmers have trouble growing crops. The change in the flow of the river has decreased fish populations.

It has also disrupted the habitat of many other plants and animals. Some plants and animals may adapt well to changes in their habitat. These species have the best chance for survival.

▶ **CAUSE AND EFFECT** **What are two benefits of the Aswan Dam?**

Natural and Human Threats

Humans can be one of the biggest threats to the survival of a species (SPEE sheez). A **species** is a group of living things that produces living things of the same kind. At one time in America, passenger pigeons numbered in the millions. Humans killed so many of this species of bird that it became extinct (ihk STIHNGKT). When a species becomes **extinct**, it means the last member of that species has died.

Sometimes a species can be saved before it becomes extinct. Huge herds of American bison (BY suhn) once roamed the plains. They, too, were hunted to the point that they were almost extinct, or endangered. The remaining bison were put into protected parks and reserves.

Some animals **migrate** (MY-grayt), or move to another region, when seasons change and food becomes scarce. Migrating animals face natural and human barriers. Natural barriers include mountain ranges. Some migrating birds will not cross mountains. Human barriers include highways. Migrating caribou usually will not cross highways.

▶ **CAUSE AND EFFECT** **Name one threat to an organism's survival.**

◀ Martha was the last known passenger pigeon. She died in 1914.

As many as 30 million American bison once lived in North America. In 1890 there were only 750 left. The population has increased to about half a million today. ▼

Visual Summary

 All living things cause changes in their environment.

 Changes in a habitat, including changes made by humans, can have both good and bad effects.

There are human and natural threats to the survival of living things.

LINKS for Home and School

MATH **Find the Number of Panthers** The Florida panther faces many threats to survival, including habitat loss. Current laws and human efforts are helping to protect these animals. In 1990, there were only about 40 Florida panthers. By 2000 that number had increased to about 70. Suppose there are about 100 panthers by 2010. If this pattern continues, about how many Florida panthers would there be by 2020?

SOCIAL STUDIES **Write a Law**

All states have laws to prevent people from damaging the environment. Imagine you are an environmental scientist. Write a law that will protect some part of the environment in your state.

Review

1 **MAIN IDEA** Describe some things that can threaten the survival of a species.

2 **VOCABULARY** Use the term *extinct* in a sentence.

3 **READING SKILL: Cause and Effect** What positive and negative effects would building a new power plant have for different organisms?

4 **CRITICAL THINKING: Analyze** Animals adapt better to a change than plants. Give reasons why you agree or disagree with this statement.

5 **INQUIRY SKILL: Compare** Use an example to explain how a threat to a species from natural causes differs from a threat that is caused by humans.

 TEST PREP
Which of the following is NOT a benefit of the Aswan Dam?

A. improved travel

B. enriched soil along the river

C. provides electrical power

D. holds back flood water

 Technology
Visit **www.eduplace.com/scp/** to learn more about threats to survival.

B71

Environmental Conservation

To protect the natural beauty of the United States, people in the mid-1800s began the conservation movement. They wrote books and articles about their concerns. They feared that wilderness areas would be overrun with farms, train tracks, and other development.

Their hard work began to pay off. In 1872, Yellowstone National Park was created in Wyoming. In 1916, the National Park Service was created. This agency oversees over 400 national parks, recreation areas, and historic monuments.

In 1973, the Endangered Species Act was signed. It created a list of plants and animals that have federal protection.

Yellowstone National Park The first national park in the world is created.

Sierra Club John Muir forms the Sierra Club to protect wilderness areas.

Everglades National Park Due mainly to Marjory Stoneman Douglas, Everglades National Park is created.

| 1872 | 1892 | 1947 |

John Muir

Marjory Stoneman Douglas

"Everybody needs beauty as well as bread, places to play in . . . , where Nature may heal and cheer and give strength to body and soul alike."
—John Muir

First Earth Day Twenty million people take part in activities and demonstrations on behalf of the environment.

Bald Eagles Since increasing from fewer than 1,000 to more than 15,000, bald eagles may be removed from the endangered species list.

1970

2004

Sharing Ideas

1. **READING CHECK** What were the people who started the conservation movement concerned about?

2. **WRITE ABOUT IT** What is the Endangered Species Act, and how did it help the bald eagle?

3. **TALK ABOUT IT** Discuss what you think the world might be like today without the conservation movement.

What Do Fossils Tell About the Past?

Traces of a long-dead animal are discovered in rock. What type of animal was it and when did it die? Scientists try to answer these questions. They study the remains of plants and animals that lived long ago. They hope to learn more about these organisms and about the history of the Earth.

PREPARE TO INVESTIGATE

Inquiry Skill

Infer When you infer, you use facts you know and observations you have made to draw a conclusion.

Materials

- modeling clay
- small object (shell, leaf, twig)
- hand lens

Science and Math Toolbox

For step 3, review **Using a Hand Lens** on page H2.

Make a Fossil

Procedure

1 **Use Models** Make a model of a fossil (FAHS uhl). A **fossil** is the remains, or traces, of a living thing preserved in some way. Mold a piece of clay into a thick, flat layer. Press an object into the clay until the object makes an imprint. Carefully remove the object.

STEP 1

2 Exchange imprints with a partner. Do not let your partner see the object that you used to make the imprint.

3 **Record Data** Use a hand lens to look closely at your partner's imprint. Record your observations of the imprint in your *Science Notebook*.

STEP 2

4 **Infer** Based on your observations, try to identify the object that was used to make your partner's imprint.

5 **Use Models** Now exchange objects with your partner. Record the similarities and differences between your partner's object and the imprint made from it. Think about what can be seen from the imprint and what cannot.

STEP 3

Conclusion

1. **Infer** What clues about organisms can scientists learn from studying fossils?

2. **Compare** How is studying a live organism different from studying a fossil imprint?

Investigate More!

Research Use the library or Internet to find out what types of fossils have been found in your area. Write a brief report about what has been learned by studying these fossils.

Fossils

VOCABULARY

era	p. B79
fossil	p. B75
paleontologist	p. B77

READING SKILL

Compare and Contrast
Use the chart to show the differences and similarities between a fossil and a living organism.

MAIN IDEA Scientists study fossils to learn about the history of Earth and its organisms.

Why Scientists Study Fossils

How do scientists know what Earth was like millions of years ago? Studying fossils (FAHS-uhlz) gives them some clues. A **fossil** is the preserved traces and remains of an organism that lived long ago. Fossils can include bones, teeth, shells, and imprints, or impressions of organisms that were pressed into mud and sand.

In studying fossils, scientists learn how organisms of long ago lived, what they looked like, and what they ate. The shape of a dinosaur's teeth can tell scientists something about what food that dinosaur ate. What kind of food do you think that a dinosaur with sharp teeth might have eaten?

fossil tree fern

◄ This fossil is from a giant tree fern that lived about 300 million years ago. It looks similar to ferns that exist today.

modern fern

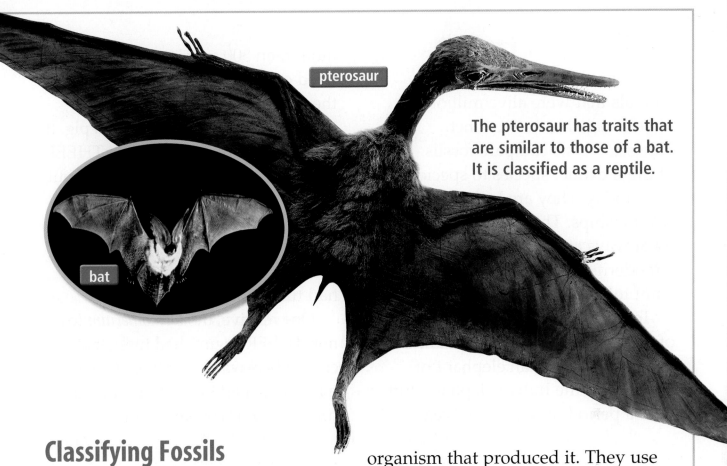

pterosaur

bat

The pterosaur has traits that are similar to those of a bat. It is classified as a reptile.

Classifying Fossils

A scientist who studies fossils is called a **paleontologist** (pay-lee ahn TAHL uh jihst). Part of a paleontologist's job is to classify organisms from their fossils. Fossils are often only part of the remains of an ancient organism. For this reason, classifying fossils can be difficult.

A paleontologist uses what is known about today's plants and animals to study fossils. Some clues tell the scientists how long ago an organism lived. For example, how deep a fossil is found in a layer of rock can be a clue to its age. Other clues can tell what an organism looked like or how it behaved.

Scientists gather as many facts as they can about the fossil and the organism that produced it. They use these facts to make a hypothesis. As they gather more facts, they may later change their hypothesis.

Compare the pterosaur (TEHR-uh sawr) and the bat shown. You can see ways that they are alike. The pterosaur's wings were tough and leathery like a bat's wings. Some of the pterosaur's body structures were similar to those of birds. Other structures were like those of reptiles. Because no evidence of feathers has been found on any pterosaur fossils, the pterosaur is classified as a flying reptile.

▶ **COMPARE AND CONTRAST** How was a pterosaur like a bat? How was it different?

Fossils and the Present

Most species of plants and animals that were alive millions of years ago are now extinct. Paleontologists compare fossils of these extinct species to species alive today. They are looking for relationships. They want to know in what ways an extinct species is like a modern-day species. They also want to know how it is different.

Today there are only three species of elephant—the forest elephant of Africa, the savannah elephant of Africa, and the Indian elephant. But over a period of millions of years, more than 300 species of elephant lived on Earth. Believe it or not, the earliest known relative of the modern elephant looked like a pig. It was the *Moeritherium* (meer ih THEER ee- uhm), an animal that lived about 60 million years ago.

The *Phiomia* (fee OH mee uh), another relative of today's elephant, lived about 30 million years ago. It had tusks and a small trunk.

One relative, the *Deinotherium* (dy-noh THEER ee um) had tusks that curved backward. Another, the woolly mammoth, had huge, long, curved tusks and was covered with fur.

▲ The *Phiomia* is an early ancestor of the elephant.

Dating Fossils

How do paleontologists date, or find the age of, these fossils? Paleontologists date fossils in different ways. Measuring how much carbon is in a fossil containing bone can indicate the fossil's age. Scientists also look at how deeply a fossil is buried within layers of rock. The deeper a fossil is buried, the older it is likely to be.

Scientists have made a timeline, called the geologic (jee uh LAH-jihk) time scale. It shows important events in Earth's history and gives information about the kinds of organisms that have lived at different times. A very simple version of the geologic time scale is shown here.

The time scale is broken down into sections called eras (IHR uhz). An **era** is a major division of time. Each era lasted many millions of years. An era is defined by events that took place during that time.

In the Mesozoic (mehz uh ZOH-ihk) era, reptiles such as dinosaurs roamed the Earth. In the Cenozoic (see nuh ZOH ihk) era, many mammals, including humans, began to appear. As paleontologists classify fossils, they add more and more organisms to the scale.

▶ **COMPARE AND CONTRAST** Compare the types of animals that lived in the Cenozoic Era and the Mesozoic Era.

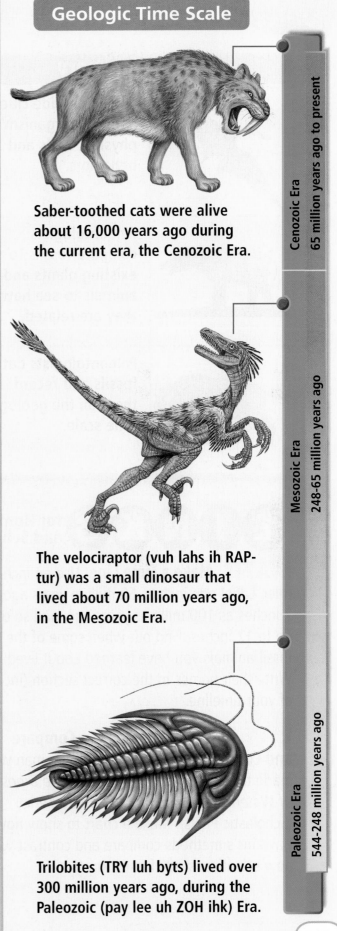

Geologic Time Scale

Saber-toothed cats were alive about 16,000 years ago during the current era, the Cenozoic Era.

The velociraptor (vuh lahs ih RAP-tur) was a small dinosaur that lived about 70 million years ago, in the Mesozoic Era.

Trilobites (TRY luh byts) lived over 300 million years ago, during the Paleozoic (pay lee uh ZOH ihk) Era.

Cenozoic Era
65 million years ago to present

Mesozoic Era
248-65 million years ago

Paleozoic Era
544-248 million years ago

Visual Summary

Fossils provide clues about an organism's physical traits and behaviors.

Paleontologists compare fossils to existing plants and animals to see how they are related.

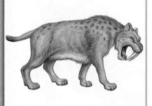
Paleontologists date fossils and record them on the geologic time scale.

LINKS for Home and School

MATH **Make a Time Line** Use an inch ruler. Label one inch as 50 million years ago, 2 inches as 100 millions years ago, and so on up to 12 inches. Find out when some of the fossil animals you have learned about lived. Write their names in the correct section (inch) of your timeline.

LITERATURE **Make a Compare and Contrast Chart** Read about the man who made the first dinosaur models in *The Dinosaurs of Waterhouse Hawkins* by Barbara Kerley (Scholastic Press). Make a chart to show how Hawkins's methods compare and contrast with how scientists study fossils today.

Review

1 MAIN IDEA Why do paleontologists study fossils?

2 VOCABULARY Use the term *fossil* in a sentence that tells one way they form.

3 READING SKILL: Compare and Contrast Describe the similarities and differences between the *Phiomia* and the modern elephant.

4 CRITICAL THINKING: Analyze An ancient animal is classified as a carnivore. What fossil clues might lead scientists to that conclusion?

5 INQUIRY SKILL: Infer Paleontologists discover the fossils of two animals in layers of rock. Fossil A is in a deeper layer of rock than Fossil B. What can you infer about the relative ages of Fossil A and Fossil B?

 TEST PREP
Paleontologists compare fossils with animals that are alive today to learn if they are ___.

A. trilobites

B. on the geologic time scale

C. related

D. dinosaurs

 Technology
Visit **www.eduplace.com/scp/** to learn more about fossils.

Landscaper

Have you ever passed a golf course and noticed the beautiful green grass and neatly trimmed shrubs? Professional landscapers have been busy. Landscapers keep lawns healthy, bushes pruned, and flowers blooming. Landscapers also maintain the grounds at athletic stadiums, office parks, college campuses, botanical gardens, and homes.

What It Takes!

- A high-school diploma
- Curiosity about all kinds of plants
- The physical strength to maintain landscapes

Park Ranger

Park rangers work in city, state, and national parks all across the country. They help protect wildlife, rescue lost hikers, and educate the public about nature and conservation. They also patrol trails and study wildlife behavior.

What It Takes!

- A degree in history, geography, or natural science
- Volunteer work or internship in a park

Master of Disguise

Can a blob of seaweed grin? No, you're looking at a goosefish. This flat, shaggy fish has the perfect camouflage for its ocean-floor habitat. It can hide from predators and be a predator by blending with its surroundings.

Happily for the goosefish, other fish rarely notice its spooky face. They're too interested in another remarkable adaptation of this creature. Attached to a spike on its head is something that looks like a worm. When other fish come near this wiggling bait, the goosefish opens its big mouth and gulps them down in a flash!

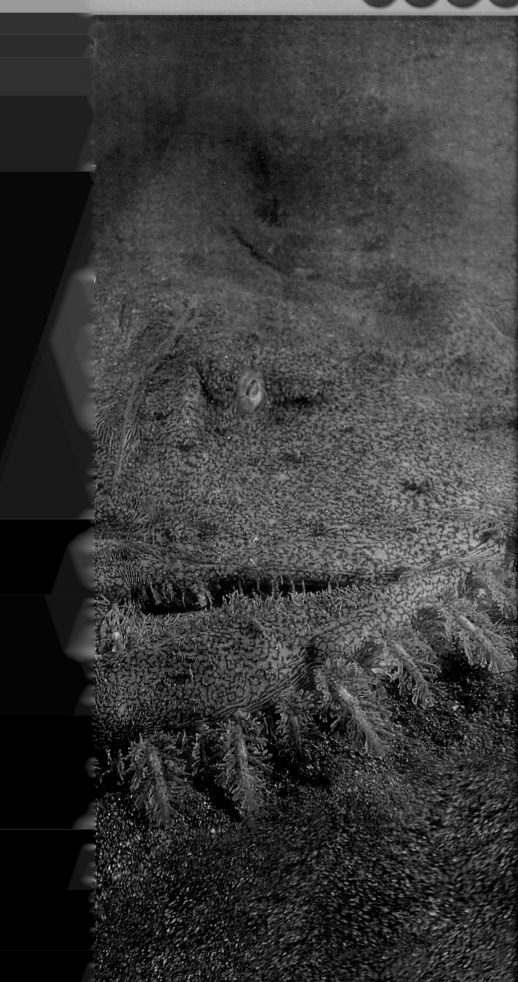

Can You Find Me?

Bugs, beware! The goldenrod spider turns itself yellow or white to match its flowery hunting ground.

Hey! Some of those leaves have legs! You can see them, but predators of this praying mantis usually can't.

Pink disguise! The pygmy seahorse blends safely into the branches of the gorgonian coral it resembles.

Vocabulary

Complete each sentence with a term from the list.

1. A scientist who studies fossils is a/an _____.

2. The place where an organism lives is called its _____.

3. Each major division of the geologic time scale is a/an _____.

4. An animal that goes into a deep sleep which helps it survive the winter is said to _____.

5. To help them hide, some animals have _____.

6. To move to another region when seasons change is to _____.

7. When the last member of a species dies, the species has become _____.

8. The role of an organism in its environment is its _____.

9. Something that helps an organism survive is called a/an _____.

10. The preserved traces and remains of an organism that lived long ago is called a/an _____.

adaptation B60
camouflage B62
era B79
extinct B70
fossil B76
habitat B60
hibernate B64
migrate B70
mimicry B63
niche B60
paleontologist B77
species B70

Test Prep

Write the letter of the best answer choice.

11. A butterfly has markings on its wings that resemble owl eyes. The markings are an example of _____.

   A. camouflage.   **C.** mimicry.
   B. hibernation.   **D.** migration.

12. Organisms that produce living things of the same kind belong to the same group called a/an _____.

   A. species.   **C.** environment.
   B. habitat.   **D.** ecosystem.

13. Which of the following does NOT describe a niche?

   A. Raccoons eat berries.
   B. Robins build nests.
   C. A desert is a dry place.
   D. Lions are carnivores.

14. A paleontologist's work includes all of the following EXCEPT _____.

   A. classifying fossils.   **C.** making fossils.
   B. dating fossils.   **D.** comparing fossils.

15. **Observe** A paleontologist studies a dinosaur fossil and concludes that the dinosaur ate plants. What observations might have led the paleontologist to this conclusion?

16. **Compare** Compare camouflage and mimicry. How are they alike? How are they different? Give an example of each.

Map the Concept

Use the terms from the list to complete the concept map.

behavior   habitats
bones   shells
food sources   teeth

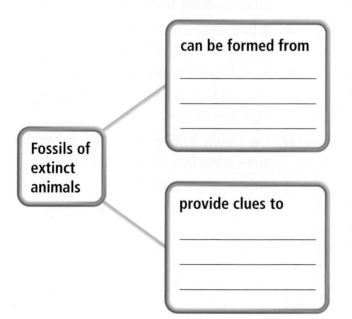

can be formed from

_____
_____
_____

Fossils of extinct animals

provide clues to

_____
_____
_____

Critical Thinking

17. **Evaluate** Two birds live in the same environment. One kind of bird eats berries and nuts. The other kind of bird eats mice and rabbits. Someone says that the birds occupy the same niche. Is this statement correct? Why or why not?

18. **Synthesize** Identify two adaptations that different organisms use to protect themselves from predators.

19. **Apply** How might an ecosystem change if an animal that eats insects becomes extinct?

20. **Evaluate** Suppose a dam is built to stop flooding. In addition to flood control, what helpful effect might result? What harmful effect might also result?

Performance Assessment

Write a Newspaper Article
Imagine that an explorer finds an animal that has never before been seen by humans. You are a newspaper reporter writing about the newly discovered animal. Where was the animal found? What physical and behavioral adaptations help it survive in its environment? Does the organism face any threats of survival? Write a short newspaper article that answers these questions.

Write the letter of the best answer choice.

1. Which is an example of a population?

   A. the type of soil in a rainforest

   B. all the pebbles in a desert

   C. all the rabbits living in a forest

   D. the amount of rainfall in a prairie

2. Which ecosystem is likely to have the FEWEST number of plants?

   A. desert

   B. polar ice sheet

   C. prairie

   D. rainforest

3. Which part of the food web gets the LEAST energy from the Sun?

   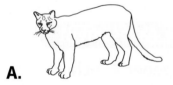
   A.

   B.

   C.

   D.

4. A plant growing far from its parent plant is often a result of   .

   A. pollination.

   B. producers.

   C. reproduction.

   D. seed dispersal.

5. By looking at a geologic time scale, you can learn   .

   A. which organisms are alive today.

   B. which organisms lived in the past.

   C. whether an extinct animal hibernated.

   D. caused a fossil animal to become extinct.

6. Which of the following is NOT an example of interdependence?

   A. Ants feed on an acacia tree and keep other animals from eating the tree.

   B. A bird cleans a crocodile's teeth by eating bits of food in between them.

   C. A bird builds a nest in the branches of a very large tree using some twigs from the tree.

   D. The clown fish lives in a sea anemone and cleans bits of food from the anemone's tentacles.

7. Which is a human barrier to migration?

A.

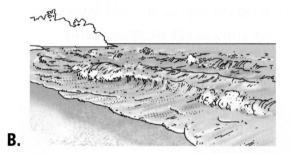
B.

C.

D.

8. Animals use camouflage to hide from
.

A. prey.
B. predators.
C. predators and prey.
D. humans and animals.

Answer the following in complete sentences.

9. The South American owl butterfly looks similar to an owl's face.

How does this adaptation help the butterfly? Explain your answer.

10. Explain how a compost pile is helpful to the ecosystem.

Discover!

A coral reef is an ocean ecosystem that forms in clear, shallow, warm water. The structure of the reef is built by small animals called corals. A single coral animal is called a polyp.

When some types of coral die, they leave behind their stony casings. More corals grow on top of this nonliving material. Through the years, new layers build up on top of the old layers. Coral reefs may continue to grow for thousands of years. Only the most recent layers of a coral reef contain living polyps.

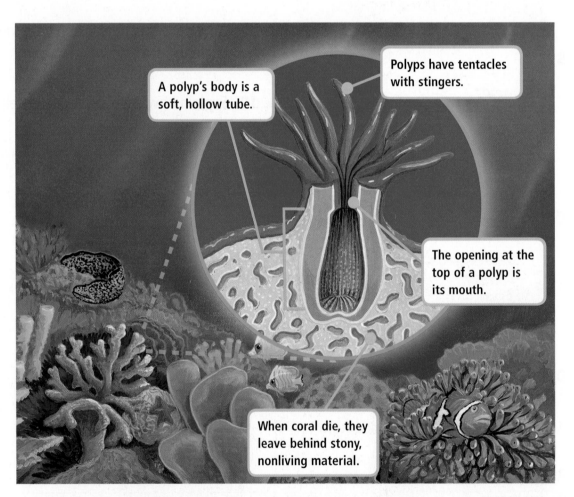

A polyp's body is a soft, hollow tube.

Polyps have tentacles with stingers.

The opening at the top of a polyp is its mouth.

When coral die, they leave behind stony, nonliving material.

Explore the colorful organisms of a coral reef. Go to **www.eduplace.com/scp/** to help a coral reef grow.

Science and Math Toolbox

Using a Hand Lens

A hand lens is a tool that magnifies objects, or makes objects appear larger. This makes it possible for you to see details of an object that would be hard to see without the hand lens.

Look at a Coin or a Stamp

1 Place an object such as a coin or a stamp on a table or other flat surface.

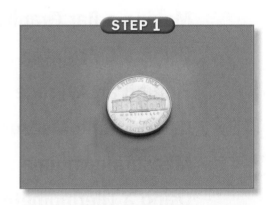
STEP 1

2 Hold the hand lens just above the object. As you look through the lens, slowly move the lens away from the object. Notice that the object appears to get larger and a little blurry.

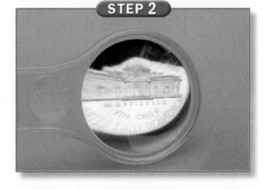
STEP 2

3 Move the hand lens a little closer to the object until the object is once again in sharp focus.

STEP 3

Making a Bar Graph

A bar graph helps you organize and compare data.

Make a Bar Graph of Animal Heights

Animals come in all different shapes and sizes. You can use the information in this table to make a bar graph of animal heights.

1 Draw the side and the bottom of the graph. Label the side of the graph as shown. The numbers will show the height of the animals in centimeters.

2 Label the bottom of the graph. Write the names of the animals at the bottom so that there is room to draw the bars.

3 Choose a title for your graph. Your title should describe the subject of the graph.

4 Draw bars to show the height of each animal. Some heights are between two numbers.

Heights of Animals

Animal	Height (cm)
Bear	240
Elephant	315
Cow	150
Giraffe	570
Camel	210
Horse	165

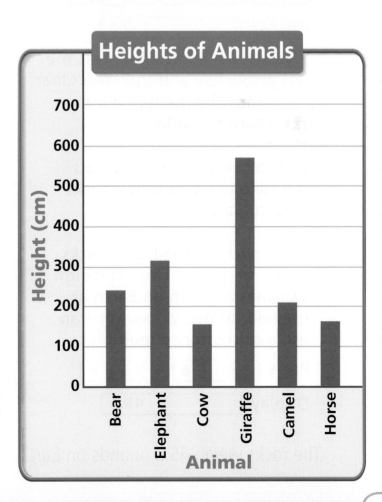

Heights of Animals

Using a Calculator

After you've made measurements, a calculator can help you analyze your data.

Add and Multiply Decimals

Suppose you're an astronaut. You may take 8 pounds of Moon rocks back to Earth. Can you take all the rocks in the table? Use a calculator to find out.

Weight of Moon Rocks	
Moon Rock	**Weight of Rock on Moon (lb)**
Rock 1	1.7
Rock 2	1.8
Rock 3	2.6
Rock 4	1.5

1 To add, press:

1 . 7 + 1 . 8 +
2 . 6 + 1 . 5 =

Display: 7.6

2 If you make a mistake, press the left arrow key and then the Clear key. Enter the number again. Then continue adding.

3 Your total is 7.6 pounds. You can take the four Moon rocks back to Earth.

4 How much do the Moon rocks weigh on Earth? Objects weigh six times as much on Earth as they do on the Moon. You can use a calculator to multiply.

Press: 7 . 6 × 6 =

Display: 45.6

The rocks weigh 45.6 pounds on Earth.

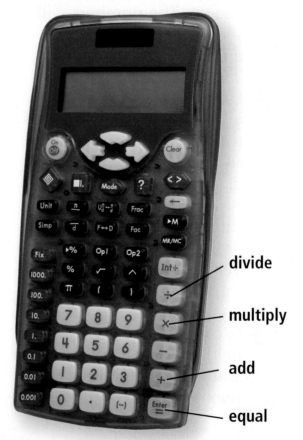

divide

multiply

add

equal

Finding an Average

An average is a way to describe a group of numbers. For example, after you have made a series of measurements, you can find the average. This can help you analyze your data.

Add and Divide to Find the Average

The table shows the amount of rain that fell each month for the first six months of the year. What was the average rainfall per month?

1 Add the numbers in the list.

$$\left.\begin{array}{r} 102 \\ 75 \\ 46 \\ 126 \\ 51 \\ +\ \ 32 \\ \hline 432 \end{array}\right\} \text{6 addends}$$

Rainfall

Month	Rain (mm)
January	102
February	75
March	46
April	126
May	51
June	32

2 Divide the sum (432) by the number of addends (6).

$$\begin{array}{r} 72 \\ 6\overline{)432} \\ -\ 42 \\ \hline 12 \\ -\ \ 12 \\ \hline 0 \end{array}$$

The average rainfall per month for the first six months was 72 mm of rain.

Using a Tape Measure or Ruler

Tape measures and rulers are tools for measuring the length of objects and distances. Scientists most often use units such as meters, centimeters, and millimeters when making length measurements.

Use a Tape Measure

1. Measure the distance around a jar. Wrap the tape around the jar.

2. Find the line where the tape begins to wrap over itself.

3. Record the distance around the jar to the nearest centimeter.

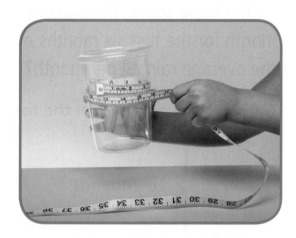

Use a Metric Ruler

1. Measure the length of your shoe. Place the ruler or the meterstick on the floor. Line up the end of the ruler with the heel of your shoe.

2. Notice where the other end of your shoe lines up with the ruler.

3. Look at the scale on the ruler. Record the length of your shoe to the nearest centimeter and to the nearest millimeter.

Measuring Volume

A beaker, a measuring cup, and a graduated cylinder are used to measure volume. Volume is the amount of space something takes up. Most of the containers that scientists use to measure volume have a scale marked in milliliters (mL).

Beaker
50 mL

Measuring cup
50 mL

Graduated cylinder
50 mL

Measure the Volume of a Liquid

1. Measure the volume of juice. Pour some juice into a measuring container.

2. Move your head so that your eyes are level with the top of the juice. Read the scale line that is closest to the surface of the juice. If the surface of the juice is curved up on the sides, look at the lowest point of the curve.

3. Read the measurement on the scale. You can estimate the value between two lines on the scale.

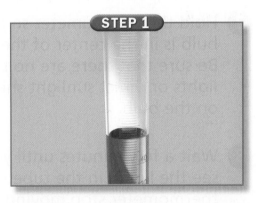

STEP 1

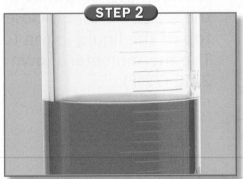

STEP 2

Using a Thermometer

A thermometer is used to measure temperature. When the liquid in the tube of a thermometer gets warmer, it expands and moves farther up the tube. Different scales can be used to measure temperature, but scientists usually use the Celsius scale.

Measure the Temperature of a Liquid

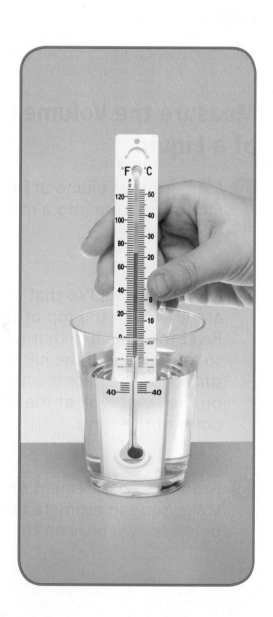

1 Half fill a cup with warm tap water.

2 Hold the thermometer so that the bulb is in the center of the liquid. Be sure that there are no bright lights or direct sunlight shining on the bulb.

3 Wait a few minutes until you see the liquid in the tube of the thermometer stop moving. Read the scale line that is closest to the top of the liquid in the tube. The thermometer shown reads 22°C (72°F).

Using a Balance

A balance is used to measure mass. Mass is the amount of matter in an object. To find the mass of an object, place it in the left pan of the balance. Place standard masses in the right pan.

Measure the Mass of a Ball

1 Check that the empty pans are balanced, or level with each other. When balanced, the pointer on the base should be at the middle mark. If it needs to be adjusted, move the slider on the back of the balance a little to the left or right.

2 Place a ball on the left pan. Then add standard masses, one at a time, to the right pan. When the pointer is at the middle mark again, each pan holds the same amount of matter and has the same mass.

3 Add the numbers marked on the masses in the pan. The total is the mass of the ball in grams.

Making a Chart to Organize Data

A chart can help you keep track of information. When you organize information, or data, it is easier to read, compare, or classify it.

Classifying Animals

Suppose you want to organize this data about animal characteristics. You could base the chart on the two characteristics listed—the number of wings and the number of legs.

1 Give the chart a title that describes the data in it.

2 Name categories, or groups, that describe the data you have collected.

3 Make sure the information is recorded correctly in each column.

Next, you could make another chart to show animal classification based on number of legs only.

My Data

Fleas have no wings. Fleas have six legs.

Snakes have no wings or legs.

A bee has four wings. It has six legs.

Spiders never have wings. They have eight legs.

A dog has no wings. It has four legs.

Birds have two wings and two legs.

A cow has no wings. It has four legs.

A butterfly has four wings. It has six legs.

Animals–Number of Wings and Legs

Animal	Number of Wings	Number of Legs
Flea	0	6
Snake	0	0
Bee	4	6
Spider	0	8
Dog	0	4
Bird	2	2
Butterfly	4	6

Reading a Circle Graph

A circle graph shows a whole divided into parts. You can use a circle graph to compare the parts to each other. You can also use it to compare the parts to the whole.

A Circle Graph of Fuel Use

This circle graph shows fuel use in the United States. The graph has 10 equal parts, or sections. Each section equals $\frac{1}{10}$ of the whole. One whole equals $\frac{10}{10}$.

Oil Of all the fuel used in the United States, 4 out of 10 parts, or $\frac{4}{10}$, is oil.

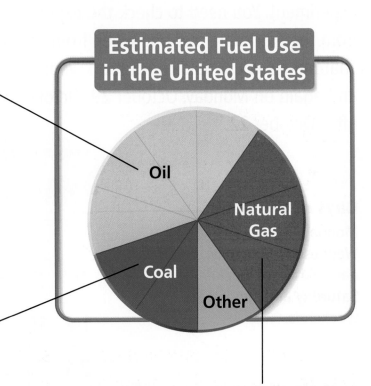

Estimated Fuel Use in the United States

Coal Of all the fuel used in the United States, 2 out of 10 parts, or $\frac{2}{10}$, is coal.

Natural Gas Of all the fuel used in the United States, 3 out of 10 parts, or $\frac{3}{10}$, is natural gas.

Measuring Elapsed Time

A calendar can help you find out how much time has passed, or elapsed, in days or weeks. A clock can help you see how much time has elapsed in hours and minutes. A clock with a second hand or a stopwatch can help you find out how many seconds have elapsed.

Using a Calendar to Find Elapsed Days

This is a calendar for the month of October. October has 31 days. Suppose it is October 22 and you begin an experiment. You need to check the experiment two days from the start date and one week from the start date. That means you would check it on Wednesday, October 24, and again on Monday, October 29. October 29 is 7 days after October 22.

October

Sunday	Monday	Tuesday	Wednesday	Thursday	Friday	Saturday
	1	2	3	4	5	6
7	8	9	10	11	12	13
14	15	16	17	18	19	20
21	22	23	24	25	26	27
28	29	30	31			

Days of the Week

Monday, Tuesday, Wednesday, Thursday, and Friday are weekdays. Saturday and Sunday are weekends.

Last Month

Last month ended on Sunday, September 30.

Next Month

Next month begins on Thursday, November 1.

Using a Clock or a Stopwatch to Find Elapsed Time

You need to time an experiment for 20 minutes.

It is 1:30 P.M.

Stop at 1:50 P.M.

You need to time an experiment for 15 seconds. You can use the second hand of a clock or watch.

Start the experiment when the second hand is on number 6.

Stop when 15 seconds have passed and the second hand is on the 9.

You can use a stopwatch to time 15 seconds.

Press the reset button on a stopwatch so that you see 0:00₀₀.

Press the start button. When you see 0:15₀₀, press the stop button.

Measurements

Volume

1 L of sports drink is a little more than 1 qt.

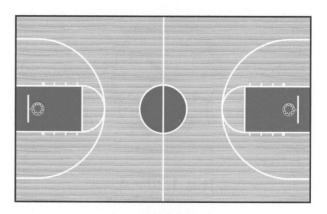

Area

A basketball court covers about 4,700 ft². It covers about 435 m².

Metric Measures

Temperature

- Ice melts at 0 degrees Celsius (°C)
- Water freezes at 0°C
- Water boils at 100°C

Length and Distance

- 1,000 meters (m) = 1 kilometer (km)
- 100 centimeters (cm) = 1 m
- 10 millimeters (mm) = 1 cm

Force

- 1 newton (N) = 1 kilogram × 1 (meter/second) per second

Volume

- 1 cubic meter (m³) = 1 m × 1 m × 1 m
- 1 cubic centimeter (cm³) = 1 cm × 1 cm × 1 cm
- 1 liter (L) = 1,000 milliliters (mL)
- 1 cm³ = 1 mL

Area

- 1 square kilometer (km²) = 1 km × 1 km
- 1 hectare = 10,000 m²

Mass

- 1,000 grams (g) = 1 kilogram (kg)
- 1,000 milligrams (mg) = 1 g

Temperature

The temperature at an indoor basketball game might be 27°C, which is 80°F.

Length and Distance

A basketball rim is about 10 ft high, or a little more than 3 m from the floor.

Customary Measures

Temperature

- Ice melts at 32 degrees Fahrenheit (°F)
- Water freezes at 32°F
- Water boils at 212°F

Length and Distance

- 12 inches (in.) = 1 foot (ft)
- 3 ft = 1 yard (yd)
- 5,280 ft = 1 mile (mi)

Weight

- 16 ounces (oz) = 1 pound (lb)
- 2,000 pounds = 1 ton (T)

Volume of Fluids

- 8 fluid ounces (fl oz) = 1 cup (c)
- 2 c = 1 pint (pt)
- 2 pt = 1 quart (qt)
- 4 qt = 1 gallon (gal)

Metric and Customary Rates

km/h = kilometers per hour

m/s = meters per second

mph = miles per hour

Health and Fitness Handbook

Being healthy means that all parts of your body and mind work well together. To keep your body healthy,

- know how to take care of your body systems.
- use safe behaviors when you play.
- choose the right amounts of healthful foods.
- get physical activity every day.
- use behaviors that keep you well.

This handbook will help you learn ways to keep yourself healthy and safe. What will *you* do to stay healthy?

The Nervous System

Central Nervous System

Brain The brain is the control center for the body.

Spinal Cord The spinal cord is a bundle of nerves that extends down your back.

- Messages to and from the brain travel through the spinal cord.
- Sometimes the spinal cord sends messages directly to other nerves without sending them to the brain first.

brain

spinal cord

Peripheral Nervous System

Peripheral means "on the outside." Peripheral nerves connect the brain and spinal cord to the rest of the body. There are two kinds of peripheral nerves.

Sensory Nerves These nerves carry messages *to* the central nervous system.

Motor Nerves These nerves carry messages *from* the central nervous system.

The nervous system carries millions of messages every minute. These messages tell you:

- what you see, hear, taste, smell, and touch.
- what you think and how you feel.
- how your body is working.

A Nerve Cell

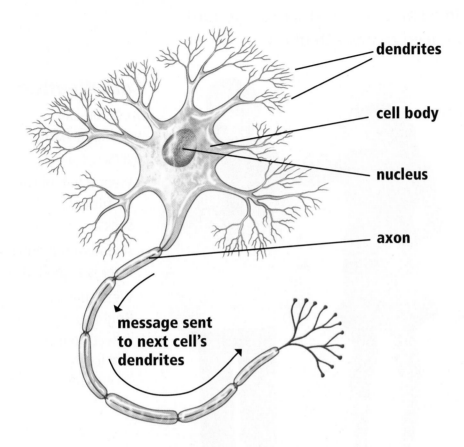

dendrites

cell body

nucleus

axon

message sent
to next cell's
dendrites

Nerve cells are called *neurons*. They carry messages to and from the brain and spinal cord. You are born with almost all the neurons your body will ever form. Here's an example of how neurons work.

1 You touch something hot. Cells in your fingertips send a warning message.

2 Dendrites in cells in your sensory nerves pick up the message. They send it to other neurons through their axons.

3 The message reaches the spinal cord.

4 The spinal cord sends messages to motor nerves. The messages cause the muscles in your hand to move away from the hot object.

All of this happens in less time than it takes you to blink!

Safety in Every Season

Being outside in all kinds of weather can be fun! But to be safe, you need to pay attention.

Hot Weather

Protect your skin from the harmful rays of the Sun.

- Always wear sunscreen with a SPF of at least 15.
- Wear sunglasses that protect against UVA and UVB rays.
- Loose-fitting clothes keep you cool and protect your skin. A hat helps, too!
- Drink plenty of water.

Cold Weather

Dress for cold weather in warm layers.

- Wear a hat, gloves or mittens, and socks.
- A waterproof outer layer is a good idea.
- Wear sunscreen. Bright sunlight can reflect from snow and ice.

Water Safety

When swimming:
- always have a buddy.
- know your limits.
- rest often.

Ice Safety

When walking on ice:
- tilt your body forward.
- set your feet down flat.
- take short steps.

Poisonous Plants

If you touch a poisonous plant, rinse the area with rubbing alcohol or water. If a red, itchy rash appears, soak the area with cold water for 10 minutes three times a day. Do not break any blisters.

Stinging Insects

Remove the insect's stinger by scraping it with something stiff, like a credit card. Make a paste of baking soda and water. Apply it to the place where the stinger was. Use a cold pack to help reduce itching and swelling.

The Exercise Cycle

Physical activity is important for good health. It makes your heart, lungs, and muscles strong. It helps you keep a healthful weight, too. It's best to get physical activity every day. When you exercise, include a warm-up, exercise, and a cool-down.

1 Warm-up Begin with five minutes of gentle activity. Walking is a good way to warm up your body. Also stretch your muscles gently. This helps prevent injury.

2 Exercise Exercise at a steady level for 20 minutes. You should feel your heart beating faster. You should also be breathing hard, but not so hard that you couldn't talk to a friend at the same time.

3 Cool-down Exercise at a lower level for about five minutes. Your heart rate and breathing should slow down. Then spend five more minutes stretching your muscles again.

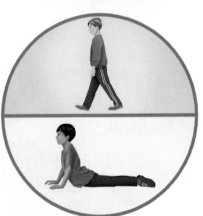

Tips

✔ Drink extra water before, during, and after exercise. This replaces water your body loses when you sweat.

✔ If you are injured or an exercise hurts when you do it, stop right away and tell an adult.

Servings for Good Nutrition

Food gives you energy. It also provides materials your body needs to grow and develop. It's important to eat the right kinds of food in the right amounts and to get physical activity. Together, these will help you maintain a healthful weight.

Food Group	Daily Amount	Examples
Grains	3–6 oz.	bread cereal cooked rice or pasta
Vegetables	2–4 cups	leafy vegetables chopped vegetables, cooked or raw vegetable juice
Fruits	1–2 cups	apple, banana, or orange chopped, cooked, or canned fruit
Milk	2–3 cups	milk or yogurt natural cheese processed cheese
Meat and Beans	5$\frac{1}{2}$ oz.	cooked lean meat, poultry, or fish beans nuts

Stop Diseases From Spreading

Sometimes when you're ill, you have a contagious disease. *Contagious* means that you can spread the illness to others. These diseases are caused by harmful bacteria or viruses that enter the body.

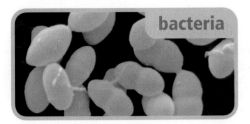

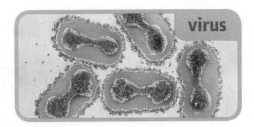

Bacteria cause...
- tetanus
- food poisoning
- strep throat

Viruses cause...
- the common cold
- the flu
- measles
- mumps
- chicken pox

To help stop the spread of these diseases, stay home when you are ill. Also do these things:
- Cover your mouth and nose when you sneeze or cough.
- Throw away tissues after you use them.
- Wash your hands often during the day.
- Keep wounds clean and covered.

❖ The Best Recipe for Disease Prevention ❖

Eat healthful foods and handle food safely.

Exercise every day.

Get plenty of sleep.

Keep your body clean.

Have regular check-ups with your doctor and dentist.

A

adaptation (ad ap TAY shuhn) A physical feature or a behavior that helps an organism survive in its habitat. (B60)

adult (uh DUHLT) A fully-grown, mature organism. (A71)

air mass (air mas) A large body of air that has about the same temperature, air pressure, and moisture throughout. (D25)

air pressure (air PRESH uhr) The weight of air as it presses down on Earth's surface. (D8)

analyze data (AN uh lyz DAY tuh) To look for patterns in collected information that lead to making logical inferences, predictions, and hypotheses.

artery (AHR tuh ree) Any blood vessel that carries blood away from the heart to capillaries. (A42)

ask questions (ask KWEHS chuhz) To state orally or in writing questions to find out how or why something happens, which can lead to scientific investigations or research.

atmosphere (AT muh sfihr) The layers of air that surround Earth's surface. (D8)

atom (AT uhm) The smallest particle of matter that has the properties of that matter. (E7)

axis (AK sihs) An imaginary line through the center of an object. (D68)

B

behavior (bih HAYV yur) The way that an organism acts or responds to its environment. (A100)

biodegradable (by oh dih GRAY duh buhl) Able to break down easily in the environment. (C62)

blood (bludh) The substance that carries nutrients and oxygen to every cell in the body. (A36)

C

camouflage (KAM uh flazh) The coloring, marking, or other physical appearance of an animal that helps it blend in with its surroundings. (B62)

capillary (KAP uh layr ee) A tiny blood vessel that connects arteries and veins. (A42)

carnivore (KAHR nuh vawr) An animal that eats only other animals. (B38)

cell (sehl) The basic unit that makes up all living things. (A8)

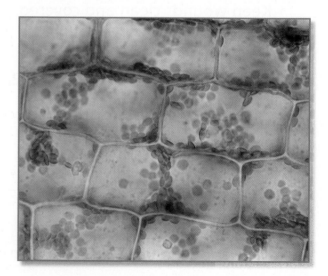

chemical change (KEHM ih kuhl chaynj) A change in matter that produces new kinds of matter with different properties. (E66)

chemical property (KEHM ih kuhl PRAP ur tee) A characteristic of matter that can be observed only when matter is changed into a new kind of matter. (E27)

chemical reaction (KEHM ih kuhl ree AK shuhn) Another term for a chemical change. (E67)

chlorophyll (KLAWR uh fihl) A green material in plants that traps energy from sunlight and gives leaves their green color. (A22)

circulatory system (SUR kyuh luh tawr ee SIHS tuhm) The system that transports oxygen, nutrients, and wastes. (A42)

classify (KLAS uh fy) To sort objects into groups according to their properties or order objects according to a pattern.

climate (KLY muht) The average weather conditions in an area over a long period of time. (D34)

collaborate (kuh LAB uh rayt) To work as a team with others to collect and share data, observations, findings, and ideas.

communicate (kah MYOO nuh kayt) To explain procedures or share information, data, or findings with others through written or spoken words, actions, graphs, charts, tables, diagrams, or sketches.

community (kuh MYOO nih tee) All the organisms that live in the same ecosystem and interact with each other. (B12)

compare (kuhm PAIR) To observe and tell how objects or events are alike or different.

condensation (kahn dehn SAY shuhn) The change of the state of gas to a liquid. (C42, D15)

conduction (kuhn DUHK shuhn) The transfer of thermal energy from particle to particle between two objects that are touching. (F32)

conductors (kuhn DUHK tuhrz) Materials that negatively charged particles can move through easily. (F55)

conservation (kahn sur VAY shuhn) The preserving and wise use of natural resources. (C61)

constellation (KAHN stuh lay shuhn) A group of stars that forms a pattern in the night sky. (D78)

consumer (kuhn SOO mur) An organism that eats other living things to get energy. (B24)

convection (kuhn VEHK shuhn) The transfer of thermal energy by the movement of fluids. (F33)

core (kawr) The innermost layer of Earth. (C7)

crust (kruhst) The outermost layer of Earth. (C6)

D

decay (dih KAY) To break down into simpler materials. (B48)

decomposer (dee kuhm POH zur) An organism that breaks down the remains of dead organisms. (B48)

density (DEHN sih tee) The amount of matter in a given space, or a given volume. (E25)

deposition (dehp uh ZIHSH uhn) The dropping of sediment moved by water, wind, and ice. (C29)

digestive system (dy JEHS tihv SIHS tuhm) One of the body's major organ systems. It processes the food the body takes in. (A33)

dissolve (dih ZAHLV) To mix completely with another substance to form a solution. (E58)

E

ecosystem (EE koh SIHS tuhm) All living and nonliving things that exist and interact in one place. (B6)

egg (ehg) The first stage in the life cycle of most animals. (A70)

electric cell (ih LEHK trihk sehl) A device that turns chemical energy into electrical energy. (F58)

electric charges (ih LEHK trihk CHAHRJ ehs) Tiny particles that carry units of electricity. (F44)

electric circuit (ih LEHK trihk SUR kiht) The pathway that an electric current follows. (F56)

electric current (ih LEHK trihk KUR uhnt) A continuous flow of electric charges. (F54)

electromagnet (ih lehk troh MAG niht) A strong temporary magnet that uses electricity to produce magnetism. (F68)

embryo (EHM bree oh) A plant or animal in the earliest stages of development. (A65)

energy (EHN ur jee) The ability to cause change. (E40)

environment (ehn VY ruhn muhnt) Everything that surrounds and affects a living thing. (A90, B12)

era (IHR uh) A major division of geologic time defined by events that took place during that time. (B79)

erosion (ih ROH zhuhn) The movement of rock material from one place to another. (C28)

esophagus (ih SOHF uh guhs) A muscular tube in the body that pushes food toward the stomach. (A35)

evaporation (ih vap uh RAY shuhn) The change of state from a liquid to a gas. (C42, D15)

experiment (ihks SPEHR uh muhnt) To investigate and collect data that either supports a hypothesis or shows that it is false while controlling variables and changing only one part of an experimental setup at a time.

external stimulus (ihk STUR nuhl STIHM yuh luhs) Anything in an organism's environment that causes it to react. (A94)

extinct (ihk STIHNGKT) No longer living. When the last member of a species has died, the species is extinct. (B70)

F

food chain (food chayn) The path of food energy in an ecosystem as one living thing eats another. (B38)

food web (food wehb) Two or more food chains that overlap. (B40)

force (fawrs) A push that moves an object away or a pull that moves an object nearer. (F90)

fossil (FAHS uhl) The preserved traces and remains of an organism that lived long ago. (B76)

fossil fuel (FAHS uhl FYOO uhl) A fuel that formed from the remains of ancient plants and animals. (C48)

friction (FRIHK shuhn) A force that slows or stops motion between two surfaces that are touching. (F92)

front (fruhnt) The place where two air masses meet. (D26)

G

galaxy (GAL uhk see) A huge system, or group, of stars held together by gravity. (D79)

gas giants (gas JY hunts) The four largest planets in Earth's solar system—Jupiter, Saturn, Uranus, and Neptune—that consist mainly of gases. (D57)

generator (JEHN uh ray tuhr) A devise that uses magnetism to convert energy of motion into electrical energy. (F71)

germinate (JUHR muh nayt) The process in which a seed begins to grow into a new plant. (A65)

gravity (GRAV ih tee) The force that pulls bodies or objects toward other bodies or objects. (D52, F94)

greenhouse effect (GREEN hows ih FEHKT) The process by which heat from the Sun builds up near Earth's surface and is trapped there by the atmosphere. (D10)

H

habitat (HAB ih tat) The place where an organism lives. (B60)

heart (hahrt) A muscular pump inside the body that pushes the blood through the blood vessels. (A42)

heat (heet) 1. The flow of thermal energy from a warmer area to a cooler area; 2. a measure of how much thermal energy is transferred from one substance to another. (E45, F32)

herbivore (HUR buh vawr) An animal that eats only plants. (B38)

hibernate (HY bur nayt) To go into a deep sleep during which an animal uses very little energy and usually does not need to eat. (B64)

humus (HYOO muhs) A material made up of decayed plant and animal matter. (C52)

hypothesize (hy PAHTH uh syz) To make an educated guess about why something happens.

I

igneous rock (IHG nee uhs rahk) The type of rock that is formed when melted rock from inside Earth cools and hardens. (C8)

inclined plane (ihn KLYND playn) A simple machine made up of a slanted surface. (F100)

infer (ihn FUR) To use facts and data you know and observations you have made to draw a conclusion about a specific event based on observations and data. To construct a reasonable explanation.

inherit (ihn HEHR iht) To receive traits from parents. (A79)

inherited behavior (ihn HEHR iht uhd bih HAYV yur) A behavior that an organism is born with and does not need to learn. (A100)

instinct (IHN stihngkt) A complex pattern of behavior that organisms of the same type are born with. (A101)

insulators (IHN suh lay tuhrz) Materials that electric charges do not flow through easily. (F55)

internal stimulus (ihn TUR nuhl STIHM yuh luhs) Anything within an organism that causes it to react. (A94)

K

kinetic energy (kuh NEHT ihk EHN ur jee) The energy that an object has because it is moving. (F7)

L

large intestine (lahrj ihn TEHS tihn) The organ where water and minerals from food are removed and absorbed into the blood. (A36)

larva (LAHR vuh) The wormlike form that hatches from an egg. The second stage of an organism that goes through complete metamorphosis. (A71)

lava (LAH vuh) Molten rock that reaches Earth's surface, such as when a volcano erupts. (C16)

leaf (leef) The part of a plant that uses sunlight and air to help the plant make food. (A18)

learned behavior (lurnd bih HAYV yur) A behavior that is taught or learned from experience. (A102)

lever (LEHV ur) A simple machine made up of a stiff bar that moves freely around a fixed point. (F102)

life cycle (lyf SY kuhl) A series of stages that occur during the lifetimes of all organisms. (A64)

life process (lyf PRAHS ehs) A function that an organism performs to stay alive and produce more of its own kind. (A6)

life span (lyf span) The length of time it takes for an individual organism to complete its life cycle. (A66)

light (lyt) A form of energy that travels in waves and can be seen when it interacts with matter. (F12)

lunar eclipse (LOO nur ih KLIHPS) An event in which the Moon passes into Earth's shadow. (D71)

M

magma (MAG muh) Molten rock beneath Earth's surface. (C16)

magnet (MAG niht) An object that attracts certain metals, mainly iron. (F62)

magnetic field (MAG neht ihk feeld) The space in which the force of a magnet can act. (F63)

magnetic poles (mag NEHT ihk pohlz) The two areas on a magnet with the greatest magnetic force. (F63)

mantle (MAN tl) A thick layer of rock between Earth's crust and core. (C7)

mass (mas) The amount of matter in an object. (E16)

matter (MAT ur) Anything that has mass and takes up space. (E6)

measure (MEHZH uhr) To use a variety of measuring instruments and tools to find the length, distance, volume, mass, or temperature using appropriate units of measurement.

metamorphic rock (meht uh MAWR fihk rahk) New rock that forms when existing rocks are changed by heat, pressure, or chemicals. (C9)

metamorphosis (meht uh MAWR fuh sihs) The process in which some organisms change form in different stages of their life cycles. (A71)

metric system (MEHT rihk SIHS tuhm) A system of measurement based on multiples of 10. (E14)

microorganism (my kroh AWR guh nihz uhm) A tiny living thing that can only be seen with a microscope. (B49)

migrate (MY grayt) To move to another region when seasons change and food supplies become scarce. (B70)

mimicry (MIHM ih kree) An adaptation that allows an animal to protect itself by looking like another kind of animal or like a plant. (B63)

mineral (MIHN ur uhl) A solid, nonliving material of specific chemical makeup. (C6)

mixture (MIHKS chur) Matter made up of two or more substances or materials that are physically combined. (E54)

molecule (MAHL ih kyool) A single particle of matter made up of two or more atoms joined together. (E7)

motion (MOH shuhn) A change in an object's position as compared to objects around it. (F82)

motor (MOH tur) A device that changes electrical energy into energy of motion. (F70)

muscular system (MUHS kyuh luhr SIHS tuhm) A system made up of muscles, tissues that make body parts move. (A54)

natural resource (NACH ur uhl REE sawrs) A material on Earth that is useful to people. (C40)

niche (nihch) The role a plant or animal plays in its habitat. (B60)

nonrenewable resource (nahn rih NOO uh buhl REE sawrs) A natural resource that cannot be replaced once it is used up or that takes thousands of years to be replaced. (C40)

nymph (nihmf) The second stage of an insect as it goes through incomplete metamorphosis. (A71)

observe (UHB zuhrv) To use the senses and tools to gather or collect information and determine the properties of objects or events.

omnivore (AHM nuh vawr) An animal that eats both plants and animals. (B38)

orbit (AWR biht) The path that Earth and eight other planets make as they move around the Sun. (D50)

organ (AWR guhn) A special part of an organism's body that performs a specific function. (A11)

organism (AWR guh nihz uhm) Any living thing that can carry out life processes on its own. (A10)

organic matter (awr GAN ihk MAT ur) The remains of plants and animals. (B6)

organ system (AWR guhn SIHS tuhm) A group of organs that work together to carry out life processes. (A12)

paleontologist (pay lee ahn TAHL uh jihst) A scientist who studies fossils. (B77)

parallel circuit (PAR uh lehl SUR kiht) A circuit in which the parts are connected so that the electric current passes along more than one pathway. (F57)

phases of the Moon (FAYZ ihz uhv thuh moon) Changes in the amount of the sunlit half of the Moon that can be seen from Earth. (D71)

photosynthesis (foh toh SIHN thih sihs) The process plants use to make food. (B36, A22)

physical change (FIHZ ih kuhl chaynj) A change in the size, shape, or state of matter that does not change it into a new kind of matter. (E38)

physical property (FIHZ ih kuhl PRAP ur tee) A characteristic of matter that can be measured or observed without changing matter into something new. (E10)

planet (PLAN iht) A large body of rock or gas that does not produce its own light and orbits around a star. (D50)

polar climate (POH lur KLY muht) Places with polar climate have very cold temperatures throughout the year, and are located around the North Pole and the South Pole. (D35)

pollinator (PAHL uh nay tur) An animal, such as an insect or bird, that helps plants make seeds by moving pollen from one part of the plant to another. (B26)

pollutant (puh LOOT uhnt) Any harmful material added to the air, the water, and the soil. (C60)

pollution (puh LOO shuhn) The addition of harmful materials to the air, the water, and the soil. (C51)

population (pahp yuh LAY shun) All the organisms of the same kind that live in an ecosystem. (B12)

position (puh ZIHSH uhn) An object's location, or place. (F82)

potential energy (puh TEHN shuhl EHN ur jee) The energy that is stored in an object. (F7)

prairie (PRAIR ee) A grassy land area with few or no trees. (B14)

precipitation (prih sihp ih TAY shuhn) Any form of water that falls from clouds to Earth's surface. (C42, D16)

predator (PREHD uh tawr) An animal that hunts other animals for food. (B37)

predict (prih DIHKT) To state what you think will happen based on past experience, observations, patterns, and cause-and-effect relationships.

prey (pray) An animal that is hunted for food by a predator. (B37)

producer (pruh DOO sur) Any organism that makes its own food. (B24)

product (PRAHD uhkt) The newly formed matter in a chemical reaction. (E67)

pulley (PUL ee) A simple machine made up of a rope fitted around the rim of a fixed wheel. (F103)

radiation (ray dee AY shuhn) The transfer of energy by waves. (F34)

rainforest (RAYN fawr ihst) An area with a great deal of rainfall. Most rainforests are warm all year, and there is a lot of sunlight. (B14)

reactant (ree AK tuhnt) The matter that you start with in a chemical reaction. (E67)

record data (rih KAWRD DAY tuh) To write (in tables, charts, journals), draw, audio record, video record, or photograph, to show observations.

recycling (ree SY kuhl ihng) The process of breaking down materials into a different form that is used again. (B48)

reflection (rih FLEHK shuhn) What occurs when light waves bounce off a surface. (F14)

refraction (rih FRAK shuhn) What occurs when light waves bend as they pass from one material to another. (F14)

renewable resource (rih NOO uh buhl REE sawrs) A natural resource that can be replaced or can replace or renew itself. (C40)

reproduce (ree pruh DOOS) When organisms make more organisms of their own kind. (A6)

reproduction (ree pruh DUHK shun) The process of making more of one's own kind. (B26)

research (rih SURCH) To learn more about a subject by looking in books, newspapers, magazines, CD-ROMs, searching the Internet, or asking science experts.

respiratory system (REHS puhr uh tawr ee SIHS tuhm) A group of organs that work together to take air into the body and push it back out. (A40)

response (rih SPAHNS) A reaction to a stimulus. (A91)

revolution (rehv uh LOO shuhn) The movement in a path around an object, as when the Earth travels around the Sun; one complete trip around the Sun. (D72)

rock (rahk) A solid material that is made up of one or more minerals. (C6)

rock cycle (rahk SY kuhl) The continuous series of changes that rocks go through. (C10)

root (root) The part of a plant that takes in water and nutrients from the ground. (A18)

rotation (roh TAY shuhn) The turning of a planet on its axis. (D68)

scavenger (SKAV uhn jur) An animal that feeds on the remains of dead animals. (B46)

screw (skroo) A simple machine made up of an inclined plane wrapped around a column. (F101)

sediment (SEHD uh muhnt) Sand, particles of rock, bits of soil, and the remains of once-living things. (C8)

sedimentary rock (sehd uh MEHN tuh ree rahk) A type of rock that forms when sediment becomes pressed together and hardens. (C8)

seed (seed) An undeveloped plant sealed in a protective coating. (A19)

seed dispersal (seed dih SPUR suhl) The scattering or carrying away of seeds from the plant that produced them. (B26)

series circuit (SIHR eez SUR kiht) A circuit in which the parts are connected so that the electric current passes through each part along a single pathway. (F57)

simple machine (SIHM puhl muh SHEEN) A device that changes a force. (F100)

skeletal system (SKEHL ih tuhl SIHS tuhm) The bones that give the body shape and support, protect the organs inside the body, and work with the muscles to move the body. (A52)

small intestine (smawl ihn TEHS tihn) The long, coiled organ where most digestion takes place. (A36)

soil (soyl) The loose material that covers much of Earth's surface. (B6)

soil profile (soyl PROH fyl) A lengthwise cross section of soil that shows the different layers. (C52)

solar system (SOH lur SIHS tuhm) A system made up of the Sun, eight planets, and smaller bodies that orbit the Sun. (D50)

solution (suh LOO shuhn) A mixture in which the particles of one kind of matter are mixed evenly with the particles of other kinds of matter. (E58)

sound (sownd) A form of energy that is produced by vibrations and can be heard. (F20)

species (SPEE sheez) A group of organisms that produces organisms of the same kind. (B70)

speed (speed) A measure of the distance an object travels in a certain amount of time. (F84)

star (stahr) A huge ball of very hot gases that gives off light, heat, and other kinds of energy. (D76)

states of matter (stayts uhv MAT ur) The three forms that matter usually takes: solid, liquid, and gas. (E8)

static electricity (STAT ihk ih lehk TRIHS ih tee) An electric charge that builds up on a material. (F46)

stem (stehm) The part of the plant that carries food, water and nutrients to and from the roots and leaves. (A18)

stimulus (STIHM yuh luhs) Anything that causes a living thing to react. (A91)

stomach (STUHM uhk) A muscular organ in the body that mixes and stores food and turns in into a soupy mix. (A35)

temperate climate (TEHM pur iht KLY muht) Places with temperate climate usually have warm, dry summers and cold, wet winters. (D35)

temperate zone (TEHM pur iht zohn) An area of Earth where the temperature rarely gets very hot or very cold. The temperate zones are located between the tropical zone and the polar zones. (B15)

temperature (TEHM pur uh chur)
1. A measure of how hot or cold matter is; 2. the average kinetic energy of the particles of a substance. (E46, F31)

thermal energy (THUR muhl EHN ur jee) The total kinetic energy of tiny moving particles of matter. (E44, F30)

tissue (TIHSH oo) A group of similar cells that work together. (A12)

topsoil (TAHP soyl) The upper layer of soil that contains minerals and humus. (C52)

trait (trayt) A feature or characteristic of a living thing. (A79)

tropical climate (TRAHP ih kuhl KLY miht) Places with tropical climate are hot and rainy for most of or all of the year. (D35)

universe (YOO nuh vurs) The system made up of all the matter and energy there is, including the galaxies, and their stars, planets, and moons. (D79)

use models (yooz MAHD lz) To use sketches, diagrams or other physical representation of an object, process, or idea to better understand or describe how it works.

use numbers (yooz NUHM burz) To use numerical data to count, measure, estimate, order, and record data to compare objects and events.

use variables (yooz VAIR ee uh buhlz) To keep all conditions in an experiment the same except for the variable, or the condition that is being tested in the experiment.

vein (vayn) Any blood vessel that carries blood back to the heart. (A42)

velocity (vuh LAHS ih tee) A measure of speed in a certain direction. (F86)

vibration (vy BRAY shuhn) A back-and-forth movement of matter. (F20)

volume (VAHL yoom) 1. The amount of space that matter takes up; 2. The loudness of a sound. (E17, F22)

water cycle (WAH tur SY kuhl) The movement of water into the air as water vapor and back to Earth's surface as precipitation. (D16)

weather (WEHTH ur) The conditions of the atmosphere at a certain place and time. (D9)

weathering (WEHTH ur ihng) The slow wearing away of rock into smaller pieces. (C26)

wedge (wehj) A simple machine made up of two inclined planes. (F101)

weight (wayt) The measure of the pull of gravity on an object. (E18)

wheel and axle (hweel and AK suhl) A simple machine made up of two cylinders that turn on the same axis. (F102)

Index

Fuel oil, C50
Fulgurites, E74–E75
Fungi, B48, B49, B68

Galaxies, D79
Galilei, Galileo, D64
Galle, Johann, D65
Garbage, B50, C60–C61
Gas giants, D57–D61
Gases
 in atmosphere, D6–D10
 changes in, E48–E49
 mixtures of, E56
 particles of, E48–E49
 properties of, E8–E10
 water vapor, D14, E8–E9
Generator, F71
Geologic time scale, B79
Germination, A65, A66
Gills, A40
Giraffes, E14, E15
Glaciers, C28–C29
Golden Hoard, The,
 E62–E63
Goldenrod spider, B83
Goosefish, B82
Grams, E16
Grand Canyon, C20–C23
Grasshoppers, B40
Gravity
 of Earth, D52
 and friction, F86, F90–F94
 of Moon, D52
 and weight, D52, E18
Great horned owl, B38–B39
Green homes, C56–C57
Greenhouse effect, D10
Grizzly bear, A72
Grosbeak weaver birds,
 A101
Groundwater, D16
Group hunting, B64

Habitats, B60–B61
 See also Ecosystems;
 Environment
Hail, D18
Hearing, A90, A92, F24
Heart, A42, A44, A54
Heat
 from Sun, D10, D24, F13
 from thermal energy,
 E45, F30–F32
Helios, F106–F107
Herbivores, B38, B39
Hermit crabs, B25
Herschel, William, D60, D64
Hibernation, A101, B64
Himalayas, mountains, C30
Hitchings, Dr. George,
 E20–E21
Hooke, Robert, A14–A15
Hot-air balloon, E1, E46,
 E80
Human body
 circulatory system,
 A42–A44, A46–A49
 digestive system,
 A32–A36
 muscular system, A54
 respiratory system,
 A40–A41, A46–A49
 skeletal system, A52–A53
Humans
 inheriting traits, A79
 life span of, A72
 traits in, A79
Humerus, bone, A53
Humidity, D22, D25
Humpback whales, B64
Humus, C52, C53
Hurricanes, D22, D28
Hydroelectric power, C51
Hypatia, D64

Ice
 freezing, D14
 melting, D15, E39–E40,
 E48–E50
 as solid, E8–E9
 and weathering, C27
Igneous rock, C8–C10
In-line skates, F96–F97
Inclined plane, F100
Infrared camera, E47
Inhaling, A40, A41
Inheriting behavior, A100
Inheriting traits, A78–A80
Insects
 eggs of, A70, A71
 inheriting traits, A79
 instincts of, A101
 as pollinators, B26
Instinct, A101
Insulators, F55
Internal stimulus, A94
Intestines, A36
Iron, E44–E45, E50
Iron filings, E54, F63

Jackrabbit, B61
Jellies, A11
Joints, A53
Jupiter, D57, D58, D72

Kapok tree, B24
Kilograms, E16
Kilometers, E14–E15
Kinetic energy, F6–F8,
 F30–F31
Kingfisher, A94

Credits

Permission Acknowledgments

Excerpt from *The Secret World of Spiders,* by Theresa Greenaway, illustrated by Tim Hayward and Stuart Lafford. Copyright © 2001 Steck-Vaughn Company. Reprinted by permission of Steck-Vaughn Company, an imprint of Harcourt Education International. Excerpt from "Arachne the Spider" from the *Orchard Book of Greek Myths,* retold by Geraldine McCaughrean, illustrated by Emma Chichester Clark. First published in the U.K. by Orchard Books in 1992. Text copyright © 1992 by Geraldine McCaughrean. Illustrations copyright © 1992 by Emma Chichester Clark. Reprinted by permission of The Watts Publishing Group and Margaret K. McElderry Books, an imprint of Simon & Schuster Children's Publishing Division. Excerpt from "The Alligator" from *The Florida Water Story: From Raindrops to the Sea,* by Peggy Sias Lantz and Wendy A. Hale. Copyright © 1998 by Peggy Sias Lantz and Wendy A. Hale. Reprinted by permission of Pineapple Press, Inc. Excerpt from *Animals in Danger: Florida Manatee,* by Rod Theodorou. Copyright © 2001 by Reed Educational & Professional Publishing. Reprinted by permission of Harcourt Education. Excerpt from "The Search" from *The Midnight Fox,* by Betsy Byars, illustrated by Ann Grifalconi. Copyright © 1968 by Betsy Byars. Reprinted by permission of Viking Penguin, A Division of Penguin Young Readers Group, A Member of Penguin Group (USA) Inc., 345 Hudson Street, New York, NY 10014. All rights reserved. Excerpt from *Crafty Canines: Coyotes, Foxes, and Wolves,* by Phyllis J. Perry. Copyright © 1999 by Franklin Watts. All rights reserved. Reprinted by permission of Franklin Watts, an imprint of Scholastic Library Publishing. Excerpt from "First Snow: A Native American Myth" from *The Golden Hoard: Myths and Legends of the World* by Geraldine McCaughrean, illustrated by Bee Willey. Text copyright © 1995 by Geraldine McCaughrean. Illustrations copyright © 1995 by Bee Willey. Reprinted by permission of Orion Children's Books and Margaret K. McElderry Books, an imprint of Simon & Schuster Children's Publishing Division.

Cover

(Lizard) JH Pete Carmichael/Getty Images. (Rock) Digital Vision/Getty Images. (Desert bkgd) Photodisc/Getty Images. (Back cover lizard) (Spine) © David A Northcott/CORBIS. (Cactus) © George H. H. Huey/CORBIS.

Photography

Unit A Opener: Anup Shah/Nature Picture Library. **A1** Merlin D. Tuttle/Bat Conservation International. **A2–A3** (bkgd) Darrell Gulin/DRK photo. **A3** (b) David Noton Photography/Alamy Images. (tr) Claudia Kunin/Corbis. **A4** (bl) Mattias Klum/ National Geographic/Getty Images. **A4–A5** (bkgd) Freeman Patterson/Masterfile. **A6** (b) J. David Andrews/Masterfile. (bl) GK Hart/ Vikki Hart/Photodisc/Getty Images. **A7** (tl) John Beedle/Alamy Images. (tr) David Young–Wolff/Photo Edit Inc. (cl) M. T. Frazie/ Photo Researchers, Inc. (cr) Francois Gohier/ Photo Researchers, Inc. **A7** (bl) © Dwight Kuhn Photography. (br) Gail M. Shumway/ Bruce Coleman Inc **A8** © Dwight Kuhn Photography. **A9** Carolina Biological/Visuals Unlimited/Getty Images. **A10** (l) © E.R. Degginger/Dembinsky Photo Associates. (r) S. Lowry/Univ Ulster/Stone/Getty Images. **A11** (r) © Bill Curtsinger/National Geographic/Getty Images. (l) Kim Taylor/Bruce Coleman Inc. **A12** (tl) Peter Weber/ Photograper's Choice/Getty Images. (c) William b. Rhoten. **A13** (t) GK Hart/Vikki Hart/Photodisc/Getty Images. (c) Kim Taylor/ Bruce Coleman Inc. (b) Peter Weber/ Photograper's Choice/Getty Images. **A14** (br) The Granger Collection. (tl) The Granger Collection. (Frame) Image Farm. **A15** (cr) Omikron/Photo Researchers, Inc. (t) © 1998 from the Warnock Library. Imaged by Octavo (www.octavo.com). Used with permission. **A16** (bl) Art Wolfe/The Image Bank/Getty Images. **A16–A17** (bkgd) Stephen J. Krasemann/DRK photo. **A18** Gary Braasch/Corbis. **A19** Peter Chadwick/DK Images. **A20** (tl) © E.R. Degginger/Photo Researchers, Inc. (cl) A. Pasieka/Photo Researchers, Inc. (bl) Richard Parker/Photo Researchers, Inc. (bc) Michael Boys/Corbis. (br) Michael P. Gadomski/Photo Researchers, Inc. **A21** (bl) Photri. (t) R. A. Mittermeier/ Bruce Coleman Inc. (br) Steve Gorton/DK Images. **A23** (t) Peter Chadwick/DK Images. (c) Michael Boys/Corbis. **A28–A29** (bkgd) Philippe Montigny/Vandystadt/The Image Pro Shop Ltd. **A29** (tr) Pete A. Eising/ Stockfood Munich/Stockfood America. (c) Roy Morsch/Corbis. (br) Lester Lefkowitz/ Corbis. **A30** (bl) John Burwell/Foodpix. **A30–A31** © M I (Spike) Walker/Alamy. **A35** (tl) © E.R. Degginger/Color Pic, Inc. **A38–A39** Stephen Frink/Corbis. **A40** (bl) Charles V. Angelo/Photo Researchers, Inc. **A41** Pemberton/Photri Inc. **A43** (tr) P. Motta & S. Correr/Photo Researchers, Inc. **A50** (bl) Lawrence Migdale. **A50–A51** (bkgd) P. Leonard/Zefa/Masterfile. **A52** (bl)Frank Greenaway/DK Images. (r) Dave Roberts/ Science Photo Library. **A54** Steve Shott/DK Images. **A55** (b) Steve Shott/DK Images. **A60–A61** (bkgd) Michel & Christine Denis– Hout/Photo Researchers, Inc. **A61** (tr) Keith Brofsky/Getty Images. (c) Jane Sapinsky/ Superstock. (br) John Daniels/Ardea London Ltd. (bl) Dennis Flaherty/Photo Researchers, Inc. **A62–A63** (bkgd) Marc Moritsch/National Geographic Image Collection. **A68** (bl) Tom Lazar/Earth Scenes/Animals Animals. **A68–A69** (bkgd) © Peter Arnold, Inc./Alamy. **A70** (tc) Marty Cordano/DRK photo. (tr) Joe McDonald/Bruce Coleman Inc. (b) Jerry Young/DK Images **A71** (l) Alan & Linda Detrick/Photo Researchers, Inc. (tl) Gilbert S. Grant/Photo Researchers, Inc. (b) Kent Wood/Photo Researchers, Inc. (r) Bill Beatty. **A73** (t) Marty Cordano/DRK Photo. (c) Gilbert S. Grant/Photo Researchers, Inc. **A75** (bkgd) Kim Taylor/Bruce Coleman Inc **A76** (bl) Bahr/Picturequest. **A76–A77** (bkgd) Charles Krebs/Corbis. **A78** T Davis/ W Bilenduke/Getty Images. **A79** (c) W. Schroll/ Zefa/Masterfile. (t) Frans Lanting/Minden Pictures. (b) Sylvaine Achernar/The Image bank/Getty Images. **A80** (b) Dan Guravich/ Corbis. (c) Dan Suzio/Photo Researchers, Inc. (t) Breck P. Kent/ Earth Scenes/Animals Animals. **A86–A87** (bkgd) David A Northcott/Corbis. **A87** (tr) Sanford/ Agliolo/ Corbis. (c) John Eastcott & Yva Momatiuk/ Natinal Geographic Image Collection. **A88** (bl) John Daniels/Ardea. **A88–A89** (bkgd) T. Ozonas/Masterfile. **A90** (bl) Michael D. L. Jordan/Dembinsky Photo Associates, Inc. **A90** (br) © E.R. Degginger/Color Pic, Inc. **A91** (tl) © blickwinkel/Alamy. (tr) © blickwinkel/ Alamy. (t) © blickwinkel/Alamy.(br) Michael Quinton/Minden Pictures. **A92** (b) Stephen Dalton/NHPA. (t) Frank Greenaway/DK Images. (b) Stephen J. Krasemann/DRK Photo. **A94** (b) © Dwight Kuhn Photography. (t) © blickwinkel/Alamy. **A95** (t) Michael Quinton/ Minden Pictures. (c) J. Westrich/Zefa/ Masterfile. (b) © Dwight Kuhn Photography. **A96** (br) Geoff Dann/DK Images. **A96–A97** (bkgd) Gergory Dimijian/Science Photo Library/Photo Researchers, Inc. **A97** (tr) Urs Hauenstein/Photo Atlas. **A98** (bl) Steve Bloom/Alamy Images. **A98–A99** (bkgd) Adam Jones/Photo Researchers, Inc. **A100– 101** (bkgd) Mike Parry/Minden Pictures. **A101** (br) Mitsuaki Iwago/Minden Pictures. (tr) Stephen J. Krasemann/DRK Photo. **A102** Jack Sullivan/Alamy Images. **A103** (cr) Lawrence Migdale. (b) Herbert Kehrer/ Photo Researchers, Inc. **A105** (tl) Jackson Smith/Alamy Images. (br) LWA-Dan Tardif/ Corbis. (bkgd) Phototone Abstracts. Unit B Opener: Doug Perrine/Sea Pics. **A106–107** © Martin Harvey/Peter Arnold Inc. **B1** Jeff Jaskolski/Sea Pics. **B2–B3** (bkgd) J. Schultz /T. Soucek/AlaskaStock.com. **B3** (tr) George Ranalli/Photo Researchers, Inc. (c) Georgette Douwma/Photographer's Choice/Getty Images. (br) Karl Maslowski/Photo Researchers, Inc. **B4** (bl) Photonica. **B4–B5** (bkgd) Terry W. Eggers/Corbis. **B7** John Anderson/Animals Animals. **B8** (t) RGK Photography/Stone/Getty Images. (b) Jeff Foott/Bruce Coleman, Inc. **B9** (t) John Anderson/Animals Animals. (c) Jeff Foott/ Bruce Coleman, Inc. (b) RGK Photography/ Stone/Getty Images. **B10** (b) Lynda Richardson/Corbis. **B10–B11** (bkgd) Michael Fogden/DRK Photo. **B12** (bl) John Anderson/ Animals Animals. **B14** (t) Art Wolfe. (b) Jake Rajs/Stone/Getty Images. **B15** (b) Ralph Krubner/Index Stock Imagery, Inc. (t) Steve Dunwell/Index Stock Imagery, Inc. **B17** (c) Ralph Krubner/Index Stock Imagery, Inc. **B19** (tr) Tom and Pat Leeson/Photo Researchers, Inc. (bkgd) Galen Rowell/Corbis. **B20** (bl) Michael Fogden/DRK Photo. **B20–B21** (bkgd) © Dwight Kuhn Photography. **B22** P. Sharpe/ OSF/Animals Animals. **B23** (cl) Norbert Wu/ DRK Photo. (b) Warren Photographic. **B26** (bl) © E.R. Degginger/Color Pic, Inc. (br) Gregory K. Scott/Photo Researchers, Inc. **B27** (t) P. Sharpe/OSF/Animals Animals. (b) © E.R. Degginger/Color-Pic, Inc. **B32–B33** (bkgd) Ahup Shah/DRK Photo. **B33** (tc) George D. Lepp/Photo Researchers, Inc. (cr) R. Ian Lloyd/Masterfile. **B34–B35** J. Borris/Zefa/ Masterfile. **B38** (l) © E.R. Degginger/Color Pic, Inc. (r) Paul Sterry/Worldwide Picture Library/Alamy Images. **B39** (l) Konrad Wothe/Minden Pictures. (r) Jeremy Woodhouse/Pixelchrome.com. **B41** (c) Paul Sterry/Worldwide Picture Library/Alamy Images. **B42** (c) Esselte Corporation. **B42–43** (bkgd) Jason Stone/Leeson Photography. **B43** (tl) Bettmann/Corbis. (frame) Image Farm. **B44–B45** Mike Lane/Photo Researchers, Inc. **B46** Jack Wilburn/Animals Animals. **B47** (b) Nigel J Dennis/NHPA. (tr) Kenneth W. Fink/Photo Researchers, Inc. **B49** Donald Specker/Animals Animals. **B50** (t) Joseph Sohm/Visions of America/Corbis. **B51** (t) Mike Lane/Photo Researchers, Inc. **B56–B57** (bkgd) © Norbert Wu. **B57** (tr) David Cavagnaro/Peter Arnold, Inc. (br) © Jonathan Blair/Corbis. (c) Lloyd Cluff/Corbis. **B58** (bl) Anne DuPont. **B58–B59** (bkgd) Brandon D. Cole/Corbis. **B60** Sharon Cummings/Dembinsky Photo Associates. **B61** (bl) C.K. Lorenz/Photo Researchers, Inc. (br) John Eastcott/YVA Momatiuk/Photo Researchers, Inc. (tr) Michael Fogden/DRK Photo. (tl) Nigel J. Dennis; Gallo Images/ Corbis. **B62** (cr) Wayne Lankinen/DRK Photo.